Communications
in Computer and Information Science

2404

Series Editors

Gang Li, *School of Information Technology, Deakin University, Burwood, VIC, Australia*

Joaquim Filipe, *Polytechnic Institute of Setúbal, Setúbal, Portugal*

Zhiwei Xu, *Chinese Academy of Sciences, Beijing, China*

Rationale
The CCIS series is devoted to the publication of proceedings of computer science conferences. Its aim is to efficiently disseminate original research results in informatics in printed and electronic form. While the focus is on publication of peer-reviewed full papers presenting mature work, inclusion of reviewed short papers reporting on work in progress is welcome, too. Besides globally relevant meetings with internationally representative program committees guaranteeing a strict peer-reviewing and paper selection process, conferences run by societies or of high regional or national relevance are also considered for publication.

Topics
The topical scope of CCIS spans the entire spectrum of informatics ranging from foundational topics in the theory of computing to information and communications science and technology and a broad variety of interdisciplinary application fields.

Information for Volume Editors and Authors
Publication in CCIS is free of charge. No royalties are paid, however, we offer registered conference participants temporary free access to the online version of the conference proceedings on SpringerLink (http://link.springer.com) by means of an http referrer from the conference website and/or a number of complimentary printed copies, as specified in the official acceptance email of the event.

CCIS proceedings can be published in time for distribution at conferences or as postproceedings, and delivered in the form of printed books and/or electronically as USBs and/or e-content licenses for accessing proceedings at SpringerLink. Furthermore, CCIS proceedings are included in the CCIS electronic book series hosted in the SpringerLink digital library at http://link.springer.com/bookseries/7899. Conferences publishing in CCIS are allowed to use Online Conference Service (OCS) for managing the whole proceedings lifecycle (from submission and reviewing to preparing for publication) free of charge.

Publication process
The language of publication is exclusively English. Authors publishing in CCIS have to sign the Springer CCIS copyright transfer form, however, they are free to use their material published in CCIS for substantially changed, more elaborate subsequent publications elsewhere. For the preparation of the camera-ready papers/files, authors have to strictly adhere to the Springer CCIS Authors' Instructions and are strongly encouraged to use the CCIS LaTeX style files or templates.

Abstracting/Indexing
CCIS is abstracted/indexed in DBLP, Google Scholar, EI-Compendex, Mathematical Reviews, SCImago, Scopus. CCIS volumes are also submitted for the inclusion in ISI Proceedings.

How to start
To start the evaluation of your proposal for inclusion in the CCIS series, please send an e-mail to ccis@springer.com.

Habtamu Abie · Vasileios Gkioulos ·
Sokratis Katsikas · Sandeep Pirbhulal
Editors

Secure and Resilient Digital Transformation of Healthcare

Second International Workshop, SUNRISE 2024
Bergen, Norway, November 25, 2024
Proceedings

Editors
Habtamu Abie
Norwegian Computing Center
Oslo, Norway

Sokratis Katsikas
Norwegian University of Science
and Technology
Gjøvik, Norway

Vasileios Gkioulos
Norwegian University of Science
and Technology
Gjøvik, Norway

Sandeep Pirbhulal
Norwegian Computing Center
Oslo, Norway

ISSN 1865-0929 ISSN 1865-0937 (electronic)
Communications in Computer and Information Science
ISBN 978-3-031-85557-3 ISBN 978-3-031-85558-0 (eBook)
https://doi.org/10.1007/978-3-031-85558-0

© The Editor(s) (if applicable) and The Author(s), under exclusive license
to Springer Nature Switzerland AG 2025

This work is subject to copyright. All rights are solely and exclusively licensed by the Publisher, whether the whole or part of the material is concerned, specifically the rights of translation, reprinting, reuse of illustrations, recitation, broadcasting, reproduction on microfilms or in any other physical way, and transmission or information storage and retrieval, electronic adaptation, computer software, or by similar or dissimilar methodology now known or hereafter developed.
The use of general descriptive names, registered names, trademarks, service marks, etc. in this publication does not imply, even in the absence of a specific statement, that such names are exempt from the relevant protective laws and regulations and therefore free for general use.
The publisher, the authors and the editors are safe to assume that the advice and information in this book are believed to be true and accurate at the date of publication. Neither the publisher nor the authors or the editors give a warranty, expressed or implied, with respect to the material contained herein or for any errors or omissions that may have been made. The publisher remains neutral with regard to jurisdictional claims in published maps and institutional affiliations.

This Springer imprint is published by the registered company Springer Nature Switzerland AG
The registered company address is: Gewerbestrasse 11, 6330 Cham, Switzerland

If disposing of this product, please recycle the paper.

Preface

SUNRISE 2024 is a forum for researchers and practitioners working on the secure and resilient digital transformation of healthcare. Digital transformation in healthcare encompasses the use of advanced technologies to enhance patient care and address the evolving demands of care delivery, particularly the transition to home-based care from hospital settings. While centering on patient needs, it also entails indispensable adjustments and advancements of healthcare processes. Whereas various benefits of this transformation are broadly acknowledged, the increased connectivity, the huge volume of sensitive health information, and the lack of sufficient cybersecurity awareness and culture among both healthcare professionals and patients result in increased cybersecurity risk and make digital healthcare attractive to cyber criminals and prone to cybersecurity attacks such as phishing, ransomware, distributed denial-of-service attacks, and malware. The connection of medical devices to the Internet, hospital networks, and other devices extends the potential for attacks, thereby raising concerns for patient safety. The COVID-19 pandemic brought attention to the interconnected nature of cybersecurity and privacy risks in healthcare. The need to enhance cybersecurity and resilience in healthcare and its supply chain has been heightened, requiring the development of new solutions. To address these challenges, the workshop aimed to bring together security researchers and practitioners, healthcare professionals and managers of healthcare to rethink secure digitalization and resilience of healthcare.

The workshop garnered the attention of healthcare research communities and fostered novel insights and advancements, with a specific focus on resilience and dynamic risk assessment, cybersecurity, and adaptive and continuous authentication in healthcare systems. The 2nd Workshop on Secure and Resilient Digital Transformation of Healthcare (SUNRISE) 2024 was held in person. The workshop was organized in conjunction with the 36th Norwegian ICT Conference for Research and Education (NIKT 2024), 25–27 November 2024, in Bergen, Norway. The workshop consisted of two keynote addresses and technical presentations, with an attendance of approximately 30 individuals.

A total of nine submissions were received by the workshop, all of which were subsequently sent for reviews. As a result of an extensive peer-review process, five papers were selected to be presented at the workshop. The review process primarily emphasized the quality, scientific novelty, and applicability of the papers to safeguarding critical healthcare infrastructure and services. The acceptance rate stood at 56%. The accepted articles encompass a diverse range of techniques addressing resilience and dynamic risk assessment in healthcare and critical infrastructures, cybersecurity, and adaptive and continuous authentication in healthcare systems. The workshop showcased two significant and thought-provoking keynotes on the topics of "Privacy Issues in IoT: Healthcare Examples from IoT Devices Perspective" by Kai Rannenberg from Goethe University Frankfurt and "AI for Healthcare Security: The Intersection of Innovation and Resilience" by Ankur Shukla from the Institute for Energy Technology, which were followed by the technical presentations, panel discussion and supporting projects' results presentations. The panel discussion delved into key issues at the intersection of child development and digital technology, focusing on autonomy, resilience, mental models, and cybersecurity for children's wellbeing. Esteemed panellists included Kai Rannenberg from Goethe University Frankfurt and Suzanne Prior from the University of Abertay. The organizers would like to thank the panellists for their active participation, critical insights, and the actionable steps they provided, which are essential for advancing our understanding and application of these important topics. The presentation of results from supporting projects featured Emilia Gugliandolo, project coordinator from Engineering Ingegnaria Informatica S.p.A., delivering a compelling and informative discussion on the EU-CIP (European Knowledge Hub and Policy Testbed for Critical Infrastructure Protection); Habtamu Abie, representing Sokratis Katsikas, Center Director from the Norwegian University of Science and Technology (NTNU), highlighting the significant work of SFI NORCICS (Norwegian Centre for Cybersecurity in Critical Sectors); and Sandeep Pirbhulal, project manager from the Norwegian Computing Center, providing a detailed and impactful outline of the initiatives of CybAlliance (International Alliance for Strengthening Cybersecurity and Privacy in Healthcare). The organizers wish to express their gratitude to all presenters for their insightful contributions and for playing a pivotal role in the success of the workshop.

The workshop was supported by the International Alliance for Strengthening Cybersecurity and Privacy in Healthcare (CybAlliance) project, the Centres for Research-Based Innovation (SFI) Norwegian Centre for Cybersecurity in Critical Sectors (NORCICS) project, the AI-Based Scenario Management for Cyber Range Training (ASCERT) project, and the European Knowledge Hub and Policy Testbed for Critical Infrastructure Protection (EU-CIP) project. The organizers would like to thank these projects for supporting the SUNRISE 2024 workshop.

The organizers of the SUNRISE 2024 workshop would like to extend their heartfelt appreciation to the SUNRISE 2024 Program Committee for their meticulous and punctual review process, which played a crucial role in bringing the workshop to fruition. We would like to express our gratitude to the University of Bergen, Norway for graciously hosting the workshop, and extend our appreciation to the NIKT 2024 chairs for their invaluable assistance and support.

December 2024

Habtamu Abie
Vasileios Gkioulos
Sokratis Katsikas
Sandeep Pirbhulal

Organization

Program Committee Chairs

Habtamu Abie	Norwegian Computing Center, Norway
Vasileios Gkioulos	Norwegian University of Science and Technology, Norway
Sokratis Katsikas	Norwegian University of Science and Technology, Norway
Sandeep Pirbhulal	Norwegian Computing Center, Norway

Program Committee

Dieter Gollmann	Hamburg University of Technology, Germany
Joaquin Garcia-Alfaro	Télécom SudParis, France
Shouhuai Xu	University of Colorado Colorado Springs, USA
Kai Rannenberg	Goethe University Frankfurt, Germany
Ilangko Balasingham	Oslo University Hospital, Norway
Maryline Laurent	Télécom SudParis, France
Nesrin Kaaniche	Télécom SudParis, France
Cristina Alcaraz	University of Málaga, Spain
Martin Gilje Jaatun	University of Stavanger, Norway,
Wolfgang Leister	Norwegian Computing Center, Norway
Fabio Martinelli	IIT-CNR, Italy
Christos Xenakis	University of Piraeus, Greece
Mohsen Toorani	University of South-Eastern Norway, Norway
Aida Omerovic	SINTEF, Norway
Hervé Debar	Télécom SudParis, France
Manos Athanatos	Foundation for Research and Technology Hellas, Greece
Sofia Tsekeridou	INTRASOFT International, Greece
Ilias Gkotsis	Inlecom Innovation, Greece
Isabel Praça	GECAD/ISEP, Portugal
Aida Akbarzadeh	Norwegian University of Science and Technology, Norway
Maria Tsirigoti	Institute of Communication and Computer Systems, Greece

Laidi Roufaida   Norwegian University of Science and Technology, Norway
Ali Dehghantanha   University of Guelph, Canada
Vasileios Mavroeidis   University of Oslo, Norway
Reijo Savola   University of Jyväskylä, Finland

External Reviewers

Ankur Shukla   Institute for Energy Technology, Norway
Sabarathinam Chockalingam   Institute for Energy Technology, Norway
Georgios Kavallieratos   University of Oslo, Norway

Contents

Resilience and Dynamic Risk Assessment in Healthcare

An Architecture of Adaptive Cognitive Digital Twins for Resilient
Healthcare Infrastructures and Services 3
   Shouhuai Xu, Sandeep Pirbhulal, and Habtamu Abie

Dynamic Safety and Security Risk Assessment in Healthcare and Critical
Infrastructures 23
   *Sabarathinam Chockalingam, Sandeep Pirbhulal, Pallavi Kaliyar,
   and Habtamu Abie*

Cybersecurity Adaptive and Continuous Authentication in Healthcare

5G Beyond for Healthcare: Leveraging AI/ML and Diverse Datasets
for Cybersecurity 45
   *Ali Hassan Sodhro, Muhammad Irfan Younas Mughal,
   and Muhammad Javed Iqbal*

A Secure Privacy-Preserving Multimodal Continuous Authentication
Protocol for Healthcare Systems 67
   Ahmed Fraz Baig, Sigurd Eskeland, Bian Yang, and Patrick Bours

Cyber Security in Healthcare Systems: A Review of Tools and Attack
Mitigation Techniques 87
   Kousik Barik, Sanjay Misra, and Sabarathinam Chockalingam

Invited Paper from Keynotes

AI for Healthcare Security: The Intersection of Innovation and Resilience 109
   Ankur Shukla

Author Index 129

Resilience and Dynamic Risk Assessment in Healthcare

An Architecture of Adaptive Cognitive Digital Twins for Resilient Healthcare Infrastructures and Services

Shouhuai Xu[1(✉)], Sandeep Pirbhulal[2], and Habtamu Abie[2]

[1] Department of Computer Science, University of Colorado Colorado Springs, Colorado Springs, Colorado, USA 80918
sxu@uccs.edu

[2] Norwegian Computing Center/Norsk Regnesentral, P.O. Box 114 Blindern, N-0314 Oslo, Norway
{sandeep,abie}@nr.no

Abstract. Modern healthcare infrastructures and services are dependent on advanced data analytics, sensing and communication technologies that include 5G/6G networks, Artificial intelligence (AI), Internet of Medical Things (IoMT), Information Technology (IT), and Operational Technology (OT). This integration incurs a large vulnerability surface and cyber attackers can exploit those vulnerabilities to wage successful attacks against modern healthcare infrastructures and services. Therefore, identifying potential vulnerabilities in healthcare infrastructures and services and securing end-to-end monitoring of sensitive healthcare infrastructures and services are crucial for achieving resilient healthcare infrastructures and services. In this paper, we propose an architecture designed to enhance the resilience of healthcare infrastructures and services. This architecture is centered around the concept of Adaptive Cognitive Digital Twins (ACDTs), which are capable of orchestrating adaptive defenses to proactively respond to anticipated cyber attacks. Our architecture has seven layers. We detail the functions at each layer of the architecture to guide the design and development of mechanisms that can be employed at each layer.

Keywords: Healthcare · Adaptive Defense · Digital Twins · Cognitive Digital Twins · Adaptive Cognitive Digital Twins · IT-OT Convergence · Resilience · Cybersecurity

1 Introduction

Advancement in technology and digital transformation have witnessed healthcare being digitalized and interconnected. The healthcare sector has a significant impact on human lives because every human needs care services [47]. For instance, healthcare facilitates a unique way to support a person with special needs, suffering chronical illness, older people, disabled, and even to everyone during the COVID-19 pandemic or its like.

Digitalization has merged with the shift to the knowledge economy, while bringing in new cyber risks and limitations to the medical field in terms of cybersecurity and resilience [16]. Emerging risks (new, unaddressed, or previously neglected) may effect resilience and continuous operation of healthcare infrastructures and services. Therefore, there is an excellent scope to analyze cyber risks imposed on modern healthcare infrastructures and services with various stakeholders and perspectives, such as industry and academia, government policy, standards, and regulations.

In modern healthcare infrastructures, Information Technology (IT) and Operational Technology (OT) medical devices are used to improve healthcare efficiency, effectiveness, and patient experience. However, these technologies face various cyber threats. From an IT perspective, according to Health Insurance Portability and Accountability Act (HIPAA) [3], 5,887 medical information breach incidents were reported between 2009 and 2023. In January 2018, nearly 3 million (50% of the Norwegian population) electronic medical records were compromised by cyber attackers [33]. This attack raised deep concerns about patients' data privacy and General Data Protection Regulation (GDPR) compliance because Norwegian healthcare authorities took one week to disclose the breach incident details. In USA, the Food and Drug Administration (FDA) is responsible for OT healthcare devices failures. In EU, European Medicines Agency (EMA) is in charge of protecting OT equipments. The trust between hospitals, healthcare providers, and patients can be effected in case medical devices are compromised. Thus, ensuring resilience of healthcare infrastructures and services is vital.

Our Contributions. In this paper, we present a solution concept Adaptive Cognitive Digital Twins (ACDTs) aimed at enhancing the resilience of healthcare infrastructures and services. This solution concept leads us to propose an architecture consisting of the following seven layers: (i) resilient users and interfaces aimed at reducing human susceptibility to cyber social engineering and other attacks; (ii) resilient cyber security management that quantifies cyber risks; (iii) resilient adaptive cyber defense orchestration; (iv) resilient cyber threats analysis; (v) resilient data; (vi) resilient communications; and (vii) Cognitive Digital Twins (CDTs), which are further divided into three types–those representing patients, those representing healthcare IT systems, and those representing healthcare OT systems. One feature of the proposed architecture is that it aims to achieve *end-to-end* resilience in healthcare infrastructures and services, where the term *end-to-end* means that the cyber risk-associated functions of the architecture are made transparent to the users of healthcare infrastructures and services. The architecture can be leveraged or extended to implement deployable real-world solutions by incorporating (e.g.) the cybersecurity mechanisms to achieve the desired resilience properties. Nevertheless, the architecture could be incorporated into other approaches to resilient healthcare infrastructures and services.

Related Work. We divide related prior studies into two categories: the ones on cybersecurity of healthcare infrastructures and services, and the ones on Cognitive Digital Twins (CDTs). Prior studies on cybersecurity of healthcare infrastructures and services include: AI model for improving healthcare security practices as detailed in [86]. This work synthesizes a systematic review of peer-reviewed literature and industry reports to identify key trends, methodologies, and challenges in AI-driven healthcare security. Nifakos et al. [54] explored the importance of human involvement in securing healthcare systems. Their research includes a systematic review and synthesis, highlighting the evolution of cybersecurity threats. Initially focused on exploiting IT infrastructures, these threats have advanced to target human vulnerabilities more explicitly. Chen et al. [9] proposed a 4-D security framework for 5G smart healthcare, considering four dimensions: subject, object, environment, and behavior. This framework aims to enhance security awareness and protection in 5G smart healthcare systems by leveraging a Zero-trust architecture. Tariq et al. [64] present a decentralized and secure method for medical data sharing using blockchain technology. This approach addresses various security issues in an efficient, distributed, and scalable manner within IoT-enabled smart healthcare systems. Obidallah et al. [55] developed a fuzzy-based approach to enhance the security of IoT-based healthcare. This approach focuses on integrating sustainable security measures throughout the development lifecycle of IoT applications.

On the other hand, Digital Twin (DT) technology has been recently introduced in healthcare and smart homes applications for cybersecurity purposes [5,61]. Specifically, [2] presents a DT-based approach to smart healthy city while using blockchain to improve data security and maintain digital trust; [12] investigates the use of generative AI to develop human digital twins for IoT-based healthcare systems; [62] uses DT technology to develop a wound-healing prediction model for treating chronic wounds and enabling personalized treatment; [58] presents a DT-based framework to achieve dynamic cyber defense in IoT-based healthcare systems; [1] introduces the concept of CDT and discusses the dynamics of cognitive cybersecurity in handling evolving threats against IoT infrastructures; [53] uses ontology to develop a CDT framework for cybersecurity. The most closely related prior study is [59], which develops a CDT-based architecture with a closed feedback loop, complex behaviors, and advanced data analytics for dynamically detecting and predicting cyber attacks in changing environments. However, this study does not present a systematic view of healthcare infrastructures and services as evidenced, for instance, by the fact that their model does not consider the IT-OT convergence in healthcare and how this convergence may bring in new threats. Another closely related prior study is [60], which proposes a solution that incorporates interdisciplinary fields including cognitive science, adaptive security, human factors, medical information sharing for enhancing cyber security in IT-OT healthcare. Nevertheless, the present study goes beyond [60] by presenting a systematic architecture for making healthcare infrastructures and services resilient against cyber attacks.

Paper Outline. The rest of the paper is organized as follows. Section 2 introduces the solution concept of Adaptive Cognitive Digital Twin (ACDT). Section 3 describes the architecture for resilient healthcare infrastructures and services. Section 4 concludes the present paper.

2 Solution Concept: Adaptive Cognitive Digital Twin (ACDT)

In this section we explore a solution concept for achieving resilient healthcare infrastructures, dubbed *Adaptive Cognitive Digital Twin* (ACDT). Figure 1 highlights the basic idea of ACDT. At a high level, ACDT aims to enable resilient healthcare infrastructures and services by (i) leveraging cognitive capabilities of digital twins to orchestrate adaptive defenses and (ii) providing synchronization between the physical world and the virtual world of digital twin for sharing security events, requirements, IT-OT health data and mitigation measures. ACDT uses a closed feedback loop to help manage, predict, and detect cyber attacks, while leveraging human in the loop and simulation in the virtual world.

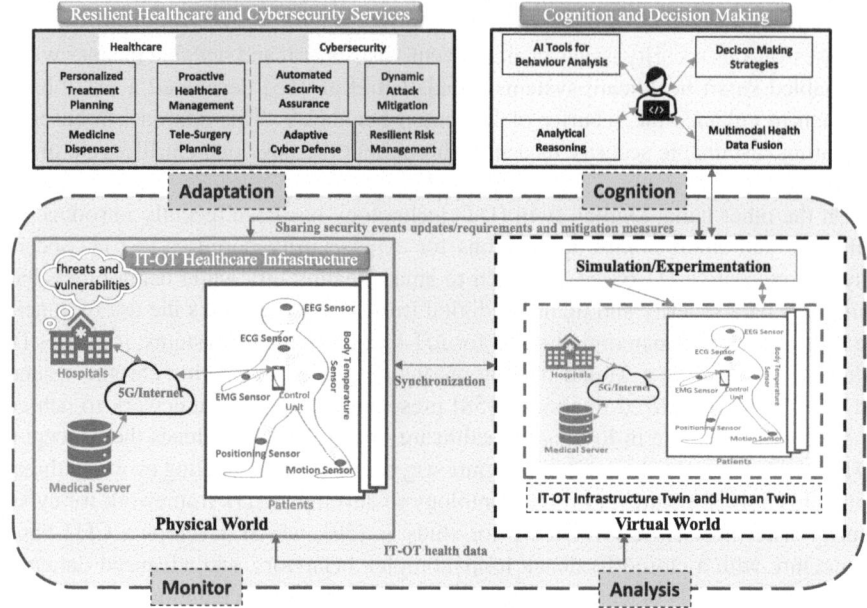

Fig. 1. The ACDT solution concept for achieving resilient healthcare infrastructures

As highlighted in Fig. 1, the ACDT solution concept has four main components:

- **Physical World.** This corresponds to a real-world IT-OT healthcare infrastructure, including hospitals, medical servers, and remote healthcare monitoring systems whereby patients are connected to medical servers and hospitals via (e.g.) 5G/Internet connectivities. This enables, for instance, medical servers to have the capability to manage the data collected from IT-OT healthcare infrastructures. The IT part is tasked to collect, process, store and retrieve data. The OT part includes physical devices and systems, such as ECG machines and patient monitoring devices. The trend in the healthcare sector is to converge IT-OT technologies.
- **Virtual World.** The virtual world consists of the IT-OT infrastructure digital twin and human (i.e., patient) digital twins, which are synchronized with their physical world counterparts. When any attacks and vulnerabilities are identified in the physical world, they will be communicated to the virtual world to help identify countermeasures and orchestrate adaptive defenses to mitigate them. In particular, the patient digital twins allow healthcare professionals to test treatments on virtual patients to understand how they may respond to treatments in the absence or presence of cyber attacks, leading to better healthcare services.

- **Cognition and Decision Making.** This component leverages its cognitive capabilities to make decisions and orchestrate adaptive defenses to enable resilient healthcare infrastructures and services. The cognitive capabilities are built on top of real-time monitoring and analysis of healthcare infrastructures and services and of predictive analytics to anticipate and mitigate cyber risks. Artificial Intelligence/Machine Learning (AI/ML) models with humans in the loop can be vital to analyzing health data and security information to comprehend potential security threats.
- **Resilient Healthcare and Cybersecurity Services.** This component assures resilient healthcare infrastructures and their services as well as cybersecurity services. Healthcare services include guiding hospitals and healthcare professionals with surgery planning, personalized medicine, disease modeling, and epidemic management. Cybersecurity services include collecting data from the IT-OT infrastructure and turning the data into actionable intelligence.

The closed loop consists of four functionalities, which are built on top of the four components described above. These four functionalities are highlighted in Fig. 2, which shows how adaptive cyber defenses may be orchestrated.

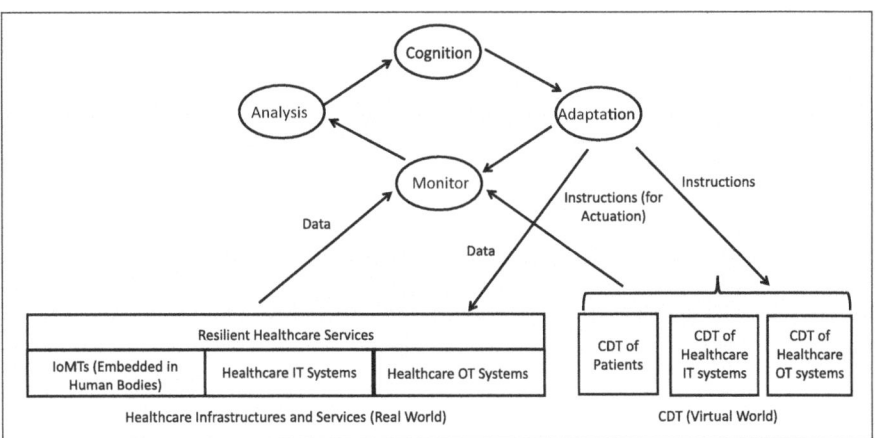

Fig. 2. Illustration of adaptive defense orchestration

- **Monitor.** This functionality collects data via the sensors deployed in the IT systems and OT systems of healthcare infrastructures. In particular, the data may be collected from IoMT devices that are embedded in patient bodies, highlighting the importance of assuring data security and privacy [34]. This incorporation of human, or more specifically patient, data is a salient factor of healthcare infrastructures because it has no counterpart in other infrastructures.
- **Analysis.** This functionality aims to analyze the situational awareness of healthcare infrastructures and service and provide intelligence for the cognition functionality.

To speed up the analysis process, we propose two kinds of analysis. One if *fast* analysis. When this functionality determines that a device X has been compromised, it will simply inform this piece of threat intelligence to the cognition functionality, which may quickly decide to quarantine the compromised device X. The other is *thorough* analysis. This analysis is systematic and thorough, meaning that it can be slow. In principle, this analysis will be invoked when the analysis functionality encounters any new situations (e.g., anomalies that may be incurred by zero-day attacks). It would be ideal if the analysis functionality is quantitative, rather than qualitative. This requires the definition of systematic cybersecurity metrics, for which substantial progresses have been made but there are still many open problems [6, 7, 10, 14, 15, 21, 46, 56, 74, 83].

- ***Cognition***. This functionality is in charge of making decisions on how to orchestrate adaptive defenses. For example, when determining it is necessary to quarantine a device from the rest of a healthcare infrastructure as the device is deemed compromised, this functionality can send commands to the relevant firewalls to filter any communication initiated from this device while blocking any traffic coming to this device. A more sophisticated cognition functionality may mimic human brain's System-1 in fast decision-making and System-2 in slow decision-making of human's cognition [50]. Note that the aforementioned notion of fast vs. slow analysis is inspired by this system-1 vs. system-2 in cognition.
- ***Adaptation***. This functionality forwards the commands received from the cognition functionality to the relevant actuators and cybersecurity tools. For example, the actuation may be to automatically quarantine a device when it is deemed compromised or automatically remove the quarantine on a device that was previously incorrectly quarantines.

3 An Architecture Fulfilling the Solution Concept

The solution concept discussed above guides us to propose the architecture highlighted in Fig. 3. The architecture considers two worlds: the *real world* and the *virtual world* with the following relationship: the real world provides, ideally in real-time, data to the virtual world, which makes decisions on how to orchestrate adaptive defenses to achieve resilient healthcare infrastructures and services. In each world, the architecture presents seven abstract layers, which are elaborated below.

3.1 Layer 7: Resilient Users

As highlighted in Fig. 3, this layer has two parts: patients and healthcare service professionals in the real world and healthcare cybersecurity operators in the virtual world. Each part will use its interface to interact with the lower layer. Specifically, one interface is for patients and healthcare service professionals to use the *resilient healthcare and services* in the real world, and the other interface is for healthcare cybersecurity operators to use the *cognitive resilient cybersecurity management* layer to manage the resilience of healthcare infrastructures and services in the virtual world. This layer needs to secure the *users* from cyber social engineering attacks and the *interfaces* from cyber attacks as follows.

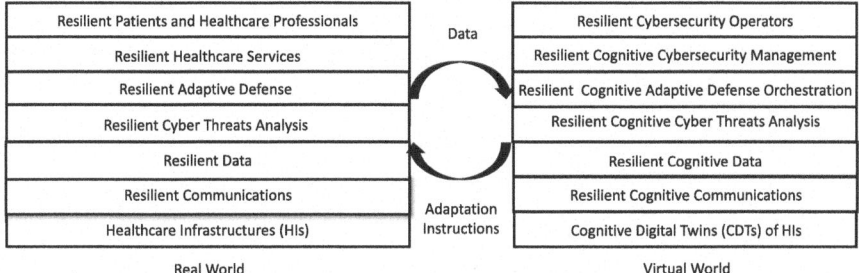

Fig. 3. Architecture of ACDT for resilient healthcare infrastructures and services

- Since users are humans, they are susceptible to cyber social engineering attacks. This highlights the importance of enhancing them against these attacks and prevent them from becoming *insider threats*. For example, a crafty insider threat may cause damages to a healthcare infrastructure and services while disguising the attack as non-cyber attacks (e.g., mechanical faults) to avoid detection and being held accountable. Despite many studies, defenses against cyber social engineering attacks have not achieved the desired effectiveness [39–42, 48, 49].
- The interfaces through which patients use the healthcare services, healthcare professionals treat patients, and cybersecurity operators defend healthcare infrastructures and services against cyber attackers. It'd be ideal that the interfaces satisfy the following requirements: (i) the interface for patients to use healthcare services should be secure and easy to use; (ii) the interface for healthcare service professionals to use the resilient healthcare infrastructures and services should be secure and in the same fashion as what they currently do, meaning that all the functionalities related to resilience are made transparent to the them; and (iii) the interface for healthcare cybersecurity operators to use the resilient cybersecurity management layer should be secure and allow them to make decisions based on recommendations made by the resilient cybersecurity management layer. In all cases, *secure interface* is important because an insecure interface may enable an attacker to impersonate a legitimate user to conduct malicious activities, which will be wrongly attributed to the user that is actually a victim.

3.2 Layer 6: Resilient Healthcare Services and Cognitive Cybersecurity Management

This layer has two parts: the resilient healthcare services in the physical world and the resilient cognitive cybersecurity management in the virtual world, which are respectively elaborated below.

Resilient Healthcare Services in the Physical World. This layer assures that patients and healthcare professionals can use the healthcare services that are provided by a healthcare infrastructure when needed. The challenge is to assure this availability when a healthcare infrastructure is under cyber attacks, such as denial-of-service (DoS) attacks and ransomware attacks. This can be achieved by leveraging the underlying layer's services in the real world, *resilient adaptive defense*, and by interacting with the *resilient cognitive cybersecurity management* services in the virtual world. For instance, some DoS attacks may not be detected in the virtual world but may only be observed by patients and/or healthcare professionals in the physical world, which can then be notified to the virtual world via data exchange.

Resilient Cognitive Cybersecurity Management in the Virtual World. This layer assures resilient cognitive cybersecurity management, where *cognitive* means it exhibits characteristics of cognitive systems (e.g., memory) and *resilient* means that it will remain operational despite cyber attacks. We propose three cybersecurity management functions:

- *Past-Threats Management.* Since cyber attacks cannot be prevented completely, it is important to cope with the attacks that penetrated into a healthcare infrastructure but are not recognized/detected until after a while (e.g., when healthcare cybersecurity operators are informed by a piece of third-party cyber threat intelligence about an attack in the wild). This could be achieved, for instance, by adopting or extending the *automated retrospective threats analysis* capability described in [30], which aims to automatically identify the computers in a network that were compromised in the past but have not been detected until now.
- *Ongoing-Threats Management.* Like cyber defenders in other settings, healthcare cybersecurity operators are, and will be, constantly overwhelmed with a large number of alerts or alarms. Thus, we need to automatically prioritize alerts so that they can spend their limited time on attending the most "significant" ones. For this purpose, one approach is to adopt or extend the *automated alerts prioritization* capability described in [25,26]. It is worth mentioning that some of the current defense tools, such as Firewall and Intrusion Detection System (IDS), do rank alerts. However, their rankings are *generic* (i.e., the same alert has the same ranking regardless of the networks where these tools are employed), and thus the rankings may be misleading. By contrast, a good prioritization scheme, such as those mentioned above [25,26], should accommodate the specifics of a healthcare infrastructure and services. This is important because, for example, an attack may cause more severe damages to one infrastructure than another.
- *Future-Threats Management.* Being able to forecast cyber attacks against healthcare infrastructures and services (in the same fashion as weather forecasting) would allow healthcare cybersecurity operators to employ proactive defense, such as paying particular attention to traffic coming to certain devices or IP addresses. Thus, it is important to develop, implement, and deploy an *automated threats forecasting* capability. For this purpose, one approach is to adopt or extend the cyber attack forecasting capabilities described in [13,23,24,57,63,73,74,87,88], which can forecast cyber attacks hours ahead of time (if not longer) with a high accuracy.

3.3 Layer 5: Resilient Adaptive Defense and Orchestration

This layer corresponds to the *Adaptation* functionality of the adaptive defense orchestration. This layer also has two parts: *resilient adaptive defense* in the real world and *resilient cognitive adaptive defense orchestration* in the virtual world.

Resilient Adaptive Defense in the Real World. This layer is to actuate the adaptive defenses that are orchestrated by the *resilient cognitive adaptive defense orchestration* layer in the virtual world. Examples of actuation include: changing cybersecurity policies (e.g., dynamically making firewalls to filter certain traffic) and deploying new cyber defense tools. We stress that this module should be made completely transparent to patients and healthcare professionals.

Resilient Cognitive Adaptive Defense Orchestration in the Virtual World. To achieve cognitive resilient adaptive defense orchestration, we need a principled foundation. One candidate foundation is the Cybersecurity Dynamics framework [77, 81, 82], which provides principled methods to quantitatively describe cybersecurity properties (including resilience) from a holistic perspective, by considering a network or infrastructure as a whole while accommodating the interactions between attackers, defenders, and users over time (e.g., devices can get compromised at one time and a compromise gets cleaned up later and so one). This is necessary because cyberspace, namely the sub-space concerning a healthcare infrastructure and its services in the context of the present paper, is a complex system where those participants interact with each other, while possibly adaptively escalating their behaviors. This reiterates why *dynamics* is inherent to understanding cybersecurity [77, 81, 82], including healthcare cybersecurity. Putting into the context of the present paper, the key idea is to consider the dynamics (or evolution) of a healthcare infrastructure, including its vulnerabilities, attackers' capabilities, defenders' capabilities, and the cybersecurity state of the healthcare infrastructure over time. Since there are many families of cyber attacks and defenses, we propose using the "divide and conquer" strategy to tackle the following families of models as what was discussed in [77, 82].

- *Preventive and Reactive Cyber Defense Dynamics Models.* This family of dynamics describes the attacker-defender-user interactions where the defender uses preventive defenses (e.g., access control) and reactive defenses (e.g., intrusion detection systems and malware detectors). The attacker may wage two kinds of attacks that require different modeling methods, namely "malware spreading"-like or push-based attacks, and "drive-by-download"-like or pull-based attacks (i.e., a user's computer gets compromised when visiting a malicious website). These studies lead to useful results, such as: (i) mathematically proving that under a certain sufficient condition, this family of dynamics converges to a unique equilibrium in terms of the percentage of compromised nodes in a network, meaning that cybersecurity is "manageable" under the sufficient condition and that the equilibrium can be statistically inferred via statistical sampling techniques and thus can be used to guide decision-making [79]; mathematically proving that the dynamics is globally convergent in the entire parameter universe (i.e., always converging to a unique equilibrium), meaning that cybersecurity is "manageable" [90]; mathematically proving that the generality of this family of dynamics in terms of accommodating literature models (e.g.,

[68,70]) as special cases; mathematically proving that this family of dynamics with time-dependent parameters, which reflects cyber attack-defense escalations, is globally *attractive* under certain circumstances (i.e., the dynamics still exhibits a certain pattern even though the pattern may not be as simple as an equilibrium) [28]. This represents the state-of-the-art understanding in terms of seeking *mathematical cybersecurity laws* in the most general sense, while noting that these laws are important to guide the orchestration of cyber defenses.

- **Adaptive Cyber Defense Dynamics.** Studies (e.g., [28,80]) propose mathematical models to describe the escalation of attack-defense interactions where defenders employ adaptive defenses, and show how *control-theoretic* techniques can be leveraged to guide the adaptation of cyber defense to force the dynamics to benefit the defender. For example, the family of dynamics can be used to guide the employment of adaptive defense to force the dynamics to converge to a certain equilibrium to benefit the defender, such as assuring that the fraction of compromised nodes in a network does not go beyond a 1/3 threshold, which is often *assumed* by the discipline of Byzantine Fault-Tolerant Distributed Computing [45] that however does not show how this assumption should or can be assured.
- **Proactive Cyber Defense Dynamics**. This family of dynamics (e.g., [27]) describes the attack-defense interactions where defenders use proactive defenses (e.g., moving-target defense), leading to the quantification of the network-wide utility of employing proactive cyber defenses. Another example of studies is to quantify the effectiveness of proactive defense in terms of dynamic software stack diversity [11].
- **Active Cyber Defense Dynamics..** Studies (e.g., [44,84,89]) describe the attack-defense interaction where defenders use active defenses against attacks, and identify optimal strategies for orchestrating active defense. Active cyber defense is based on spreading "white" or "benign" worms to combat malware (i.e., malicious worms) that spread over a network. The notion of active defense was later independently re-invented in the term dubbed "goodware" [66].

The preceding kinds of defenses can be synergized into various flavors of adaptive defense, such as *adaptive proactive* defense. This highlights the importance to pave a systematic foundation for guiding adaptive defenses. For this purpose, we advocate further studies on characterizing and controlling these kinds of cybersecurity dynamics as there are a range of technical barriers that are yet to be tackled [27,82]. For instance, one technical barrier is the *dependence* between random variables in cybersecurity dynamics models, which is often assumed away by most studies while it should not. Despite initial results in tackling this dependence barrier [72,75], which show that assuming away the due dependence will cause misleading or incorrect results, there are many open problems.

3.4 Layer 4: Resilient Cyber Threats Analysis

This layer corresponds to the ***Analysis*** functionality of the adaptive defense orchestration. This layer also has two parts: *resilient cyber threats analysis* in the real world and *resilient cognitive cyber threats analysis* in the virtual world.

An Architecture of Adaptive Cognitive Digital Twins for Resilient Healthcare 13

Resilient Cyber Threats Analysis in the Real World. This layer should provide the following capabilities.

- *Real-World Assets Management.* This capability is to automate the management of digital assets in a given healthcare infrastructure, including its network structure, data flows, software stacks, and services (e.g., email and file-sharing).
- *Real-World Vulnerability and Patch Management.* This capability takes as input the output of vulnerability scanners, third-party cyber threat intelligence, and the results obtained by applying vulnerability detectors that are based on code analysis [35–38,91] (which are different from vulnerability scanners). The patch management deals with which vulnerabilities have (not) been patched.
- *Real-World Alerts Management.* This capability keeps track of the alerts that are dynamically generated by the employed cyber defense tools, while accompanying each alert with the pertinent information. The information will be leveraged by the upper layer to prioritize alert response and orchestrating adaptive defense.
- *Real-World Situation Management.* This capability provides healthcare cybersecurity operators with real-time situational awareness of a network or healthcare infrastructure through a unified representation of the dynamical situation. The dynamic situation should reflect the dynamics of the assets, where each asset should be annotated with the relevant information (e.g., its version, vulnerability, and patch information). Moreover, the communications between computers should be appropriately encoded into the situation representation (e.g., which computers communicated with which other computers, using what protocols and ports, at what time). For this purpose, one approach is to adopt or extend our dynamic graph-representation proposed in [26].

Resilient Cognitive Cyber Threats Analysis in the Virtual World. This layer goes beyond its peer in the real world by conducting a thorough cyber threats analysis, such as forecasting-based analysis. This layer should provide the following capabilities.

- *Virtual-World Assets Management.* This capability goes beyond the real-world assets management by using unified data structures and associated algorithms for representing, retrieving, and processing assets information, and for answering healthcare cybersecurity operators' questions (e.g., which computers in a healthcare infrastructure are running a certain version of a certain browser). Unified representation of data is important to interoperability and extensibility.
- *Virtual-World Vulnerability and Patch Management.* This capability goes beyond the real-world vulnerability and patch management capability by using data structures and algorithms to represent, retrieve, and process vulnerability and patch information. The algorithms should answer a range of questions, such as: Which computers in a healthcare infrastructure have a certain vulnerability? Which vulnerabilities have (not) been patched? While some vulnerabilities may have been immediately patched, others may need a more nuanced defense when patches are not available or patching requires shutting down mission-critical services (which may not be justifiable despite the presence of vulnerabilities). For the vulnerabilities that cannot be immediately patched, this capability should provide alternative solutions, such as

the best course-of-action to mitigate the vulnerability with minimal disruption to the service in question (e.g., paying particular attention to the network traffic originating from, or coming to, a certain port of a vulnerable computer).
- *Virtual-World Alerts Management.* This capability goes beyond its real-world counterpart by further using *alerts index*, which provides contextualized ranking of alert importance [25, 26], to manage time series of alerts and design algorithms to answer queries, such as the following: (i) What are the alerts that are triggered by the communications between certain computers and/or devices during a certain period of time? (ii) Which alerts are repeatedly triggered today in a healthcare infrastructure? This may indicate a large volume of false-positives or ongoing attacks. Answering these questions will directly support the Past-Threats Management at Layer 6 (e.g., when it becomes known to the healthcare cybersecurity operators at a later point in time that certain alerts in the past indicate an attack that is not recognized until now) and the Ongoing-Threats Management at Layer 6 (e.g., for prioritizing the ongoing alerts for healthcare cybersecurity operators to respond).
- *Virtual-World Situation Management.* This capability goes beyond its real-world counterpart by using the infrastructure-wide *dynamic situation* to manage the situation and forecast its evolution. The dynamic situation should include data structures for representing the assets, where each asset will be annotated with the relevant information as mentioned above (e.g., version, vulnerability, and patch information). Moreover, the communications between computers or devices will be encoded into an appropriate situation representation (e.g., which computers communicated with which other computers, using what protocols and ports, at what time).

3.5 Layer 3: Resilient Data

Resilient data means that the following properties are preserved despite successful cyber attacks against healthcare infrastructures.

- *Resilient Data Confidentiality.* Even in presence of successful cyber attacks, the damage to data confidentiality incurred by these attacks should be minimized. It is important to realize that confidentiality, once compromised, cannot be recovered.
- *Resilient Data Integrity.* Even in the presence of successful cyber attacks, the damage to data integrity incurred by these attacks should be minimized. It is important to realize that integrity, even if compromised, could be recovered as long as the "clean" data has backups.
- *Resilient Healthcare Service Availability.* Even in the presence of successful cyber attacks, the damage to the availability of healthcare infrastructures (including data) and services should be minimized.
- *Resilient Accountability.* Even in the presence of successful cyber attacks (e.g., attacker hacking into healthcare service provider's data server or compromising legitimate users' credentials), the damage should be minimized (e.g., unlawful compromise and selling of confidential should not be wrongly attributed to an innocent healthcare professional).

These properties should be assured in both the real world and the virtual world. One difference between the *cognitive resilient data* in the virtual world and the *resilient data* in the real world is that the former can include "what if" data (e.g., supposing a device contains a zero-day vulnerability) and thus can be leveraged to conduct various kinds of "what if" analysis by the *resilient cognitive cyber threats analysis* capability at Layer 4.

3.6 Layer 2: Resilient Communications

This layer also has two parts: *resilient communications* in the real world and *resilient cognitive communications* in the virtual world.

Resilient Communications in the Real World. Communications must be resilient against cyber attacks, such as eavesdropping, injecting, compromising, and jamming attacks. To thwart eavesdropping and injecting attacks, it is sufficient to employ cryptographic solutions with rigorous analysis (i.e., using protocols that have been rigorously proven to be secure in the modern cryptography framework). For instance, pure eavesdropping attacks can be thwarted by the employment of appropriate encryption schemes, pure injecting attacks can be thwarted by message authentication schemes or digital signature schemes, and joint eavesdropping and injecting attacks (i.e., an attacker has these two kinds of capabilities) can be thwarted by authenticated encryption schemes. However, attacks in the real world often go beyond these relatively simple threat models. One particular challenge is deal with the compromise of cryptographic keys, which can be incurred by successful system attacks (see, e.g., [29]).

To thwart compromises of communication end points (e.g., a sender or receiver), which can render the aforementioned cryptographic techniques useless, it is necessary to use advanced cryptographic techniques. For instance, in point-to-point communications, key-insulated cryptosystems [18–20] can be employed to mitigate the damages incurred by the presence of compromised end nodes that have not been detected as compromised. In the context of secure group communications (also known as secure multicast), advanced key management protocols can be used. However, it is often challenging to assure their security properties. This is evidenced by the fact that the Logical Key Hierarchical (LKH) protocol [69, 71] and its stateless siblings [32, 51], which were elegantly designed and widely believed to be unbreakable, were found flawed and provably fixed almost 10 years later [76]. Moreover, there is often a delay in detecting successful attacks, including the compromise of cryptographic keys [43], prompting the need of systematic methods in mitigating the damages that can be incurred by compromised but undetected cryptographic keys, such as those presented in [17, 78, 85]. These highlight the challenges that can be encountered when designing cryptographic protocols to achieve resilient communications.

To thwart jamming and other attacks against wireless networks, which are relevant because healthcare infrastructures and services will leverage 5G/6G techniques, it is also necessary to employ advanced techniques. For instance, cryptographic secret sharing can be leveraged to make communications resilient against jamming and eavesdropping attacks [67].

Resilient Cognitive Communications in the Virtual World. This layer goes beyond its real-world counterpart by allowing various kinds of "what if" analysis. For instance, a thorough "what if" analysis would need to be conducted before upgrading the cryptosystems that are used to assure resilient communications in the real world to their post-quantum counterparts. This is important not only for the purpose of measuring the cybersecurity and resilience gain that would be obtained by employing post-quantum cryptographic schemes [8,31], but also for the purpose of testing their feasibility and performance overhead on the Internet of Medical Things (IoMTs) that often have limited power supplies and compute capacities. It is also important to thoroughly test advanced communication techniques (e.g., cognitive communication schemes) in the virtual world before using them to replace the previously employed ones in the physical world. This kind of analysis has a good potential in identifying zero-day vulnerabilities, enabling proactive defenses against the exploitation of them.

3.7 Layer 1: Healthcare Infrastructures and Their Cognitive Digital Twins

This layer also has two parts: the *healthcare infrastructures* in the real world and their *cognitive digital twins* in the virtual world.

Healthcare Infrastructures in the Real World. This serves as a baseline for designing the virtual-world ACDTs of the real-world healthcare infrastructures, such as the software stack and their versions that can indicate their vulnerabilities.

Cognitive Digital Twins (CDTs) in the Virtual World. We envision that CDTs will play a critical role in the future healthcare sector. Going beyond the notion of Digital Twins (DTs), CDTs further offer the cognition capability to digital twins to achieve a degree of autonomy in decision-making. Intuitively, cognition is the process triggered by some stimulus, processes the stimulus, and generates a response to the stimulus. Neisser [52] defines *cognition* as the mental processes that transform, reduce, elaborate, store, recover, and use sensory input data. By projecting and interpreting cognition in the context of the present study, we envision that a cognitive process should have the following characteristics:

- *perception*, such as the process for formulating meaningful representations from raw input data;
- *memory*, such as the process for storing information for further processing, and encoding and retrieving knowledge at a time when the need arises;
- *attention*, such as selecting a focus based on the raw input data and memory;
- *learning*, such as the process turning experience into knowledge for future uses;
- *reasoning*, such as the process for drawing conclusions to help decision-making by leveraging beliefs and observations;
- *decision-making*, such as the process for identifying a solution to a problem, which is essential to autonomy.

We envision that these, and potentially other, characteristics need to be possessed by CDTs, offering effective guidance for future studies.

To make healthcare infrastructures and service resilient against cyber attacks, we further envision the need of three kinds of CDTs: CDTs of patients, CDTs of healthcare IT systems, and CDTs of healthcare OT systems.

- **CDTs of Patients or Human Digital Twin (HDT).** HDT is a virtual representation of patients for monitoring physical, biochemical, and behavioral characteristics which can be used for medical purposes such as personalized medicine, injury prevention, tele-surgery planning, and telecare. HDT collects data from wearable and/or implantable IoMT devices that monitor (e.g.) physiological features such as temperature, heart rate, pulse, blood pressure, and emotional changes. Recently, Affective HDT (AHDT) is developed to utilize biometrics and AI for developing virtual twin of person's emotions and behaviors [4]. Human-Robot Collaboration (HRC) is a highly promising paradigm for intelligent applications. As a result, HDT can leverage highly dynamic HRC applications [22] to predict and manage Elderly type 2 diabetes (E-T2D) and precise insulin infusion [65] and identify facial expression and body movement for emotion recognition [4].
- **CDTs of Healthcare IT Systems.** These CDTs mimic the IT systems in real-world healthcare infrastructures and provide a baseline of normal behaviors of these IT systems. The CDTs can take two kinds of input: one is the *data* provided by the sensors that are employed in the healthcare infrastructures and services IT systems, which reflects their state in real time; the other is the *task* made by a healthcare cybersecurity operator. These CDTs have two kinds of output: one is the *data* that will be provided to the Analysis functionality at the Resilient Cyber Threats Analysis layer; the other is the *virtual outcomes* that is "produced" by these CDTs according to the *task* and is given to the healthcare infrastructures and services. In the absence of cyber attacks, the outcomes in the healthcare infrastructures should be the same as the virtual outcomes output by CDTs. This could prevent incidents like the recent one of Microsoft Blue Screen of Death incurred by CrowdStrike software update.
- **CDTs of Healthcare OT Systems.** These CDTs mimic the OT systems in real-world healthcare infrastructures and provide a baseline of normal behaviors of these OT systems to the virtual world. These CDTs can take two kinds of input: one is the *data* provided by the sensors that are employed in the healthcare infrastructures and services OT systems, which reflects the state of the healthcare infrastructures and services in real time; the other is the *task* that is made by a healthcare professional. These CDTs have two kinds of output: one is the *data* that will be provided to the Analysis functionality of the Resilient Cognitive Cyber Threats Analysis layer in the virtual world; the other is the *virtual outcomes* that is "produced" by these CDTs according to the *task* and is given to the healthcare infrastructures and services OT systems. In the absence of cyber attacks, the outcomes in the healthcare infrastructures should be the same as the virtual outcomes output by these CDTs in the virtual world.

4 Conclusion and Future Work

We have presented an architecture of Adaptive Cognitive Digital Twins (ACDT) designed to enhance the resilience of healthcare infrastructures and services. The novel characteristics of this architecture is its cognition capability, which orchestrates automated and autonomous adaptive defenses to proactively respond to anticipated cyber attacks. The architecture consists of seven layers: (i) resilient users and interfaces aimed at reducing human susceptibility to cyber social engineering and other attacks; (ii) resilient cybersecurity management that quantifies cyber risks; (iii) resilient adaptive cyber defense orchestration; (iv) resilient cyber threat analysis; (v) resilient data; (vi) resilient communications; and (vii) Cognitive Digital Twins (CDTs), which are further divided into three types: those representing patients, those representing healthcare IT systems, and those representing healthcare OT systems. These layers enable orchestrating adaptive defenses and resilience to proactively respond to continuously evolving cyber attacks.

We hope the paper, especially the architecture, will inspire further research on designing architectures to enable resilient healthcare infrastructures and services. Moreover, it is an fascinating research problem to define a systematic set of metrics whereby we can fairly compare different architectures that aim to achieve resilient healthcare infrastructures and services. Another thrust of future research is to adapt the proposed solution in different critical sectors such as industry 4.0, smart cities, smart grid, and transportation to validate and benchmark its feasibility and performance.

Acknowledgment. Shouhuai Xu is supported in part by NSF Grant #2115134 and Colorado State Bill 18-086. This work is supported by the European Union's HORIZON Research and Innovation Programme under grant agreement No 101120657, project ENFIELD (European Lighthouse to Manifest Trustworthy and Green AI). This research is also partially funded from the Research Council of Norway through, the SFI Norwegian Centre for Cybersecurity in Critical Sectors (NORCICS), with the project number #310105 and International Alliance for Strengthening Cybersecurity and Privacy in Healthcare (CybAlliance), with the project number #337316.

References

1. Abie, A.: Cognitive cybersecurity for cps-iot enabled healthcare ecosystems. In: 2019 13th International Symposium on Medical Information and Communication Technology (ISMICT), pp. 1–6. IEEE (2019)
2. Ahmadi-Assalemi, G., et al.: Digital twins for precision healthcare. Cyber Defence in the Age of AI, Smart Societies and Augmented Humanity, pp. 133–158 (2020)
3. Alder, S.: Healthcare data breach statistics. HIPAA J.,1 (2024)
4. Amara, K., Kerdjidj, O., Ramzan, N.: Emotion recognition for affective human digital twin by means of virtual reality enabling technologies. IEEE Access **11**, 74216–74227 (2023)
5. Bera, B., Das, A.K., Sikdar, B.: Digital twins-empowered secure network slice access and isolation for consumer healthcare applications. IEEE Trans. Serv. Comput. (2024)
6. Charlton, J., Du, P., Cho, J., Xu, S.: Measuring relative accuracy of malware detectors in the absence of ground truth. In: IEEE MILCOM (2018)
7. Charlton, J., Du, P., Xu, S.: A new method for inferring ground-truth labels and malware detector effectiveness metrics. In: Lu, W., Sun, K., Yung, M., Liu, F. (eds.) SciSec 2021. LNCS, vol. 13005, pp. 77–92. Springer, Cham (2021). https://doi.org/10.1007/978-3-030-89137-4_6
8. Chawla, D., Mehra, P.S.: A roadmap from classical cryptography to post-quantum resistant cryptography for 5g-enabled iot: Challenges, opportunities and solutions. Internet of Thing, 100950 (2023)
9. Chen, B., et al.: A security awareness and protection system for 5g smart healthcare based on zero-trust architecture. IEEE Internet Things J. **8**(13), 10248–10263 (2020)

10. Chen, H., Cho, J., Xu, S.: Quantifying the security effectiveness of firewalls and dmzs. In: Proceedings of HoTSoS 2018, pp. 9:1–9:11 (2018)
11. Huashan, C., Hasan, C., Xu, S.: Quantifying cybersecurity effectiveness of dynamic network diversity. IEEE Trans. Dependable Sec. Comput. (2021)
12. Chen, J., Shi, Y., Yi, C., Du, H., Kang, J., Niyato, D.: Generative ai-driven human digital twin in iot-healthcare: A comprehensive survey. arXiv preprint arXiv:2401.13699 (2024)
13. Chen, Y., Huang, Z., Xu, S., Lai, Y.: Spatiotemporal patterns and predictability of cyberattacks. PLoS ONE **10**(5), e0124472 (2015)
14. Cho, J., Hurley, P., Xu, S.: Metrics and measurement of trustworthy systems. In: Proc, IEEE MILCOM (2016)
15. Cho, J.-H., Xu, S., Hurley, P.M., Mackay, M., Benjamin, T., Beaumont, M.: Stram: measuring the trustworthiness of computer-based systems. ACM Comput. Surv., **51**(6):128:1–128:47, (2019)
16. Cobianchi, L., et al.: Planning the full recovery phase: an antifragile perspective on surgery after covid-19. Ann. Surg. **272**(6), e296–e299 (2020)
17. Dai, W., Parker, P., Jin, H., Xu, S.: Enhancing data trustworthiness via assured digital signing. IEEE TDSC **9**(6), 838–851 (2012)
18. Dodis, Y., Katz, J., Xu, S., Yung, M.: Key-insulated public key cryptosystems. In: Knudsen, L.R. (ed.) EUROCRYPT 2002. LNCS, vol. 2332, pp. 65–82. Springer, Heidelberg (2002). https://doi.org/10.1007/3-540-46035-7_5
19. Dodis, Y., Katz, J., Xu, S., Yung, M.: Strong key-insulated signature schemes. In: Public Key Cryptography (PKC 2003), pp. 130–144 (2003)
20. Dodis, Y., Luo, W., Xu, S., Yung, M.: Key-insulated symmetric key cryptography and mitigating attacks against cryptographic cloud software. In: Proceeding of ASIACCS 2012 (2012)
21. Du, P., Sun, Z., Chen, H., Cho, J.H., Xu, S.: Statistical estimation of malware detection metrics in the absence of ground truth. IEEE T-IFS **13**(12), 2965–2980 (2018)
22. Fan, J., Zheng, P., Lee, C.K.M.: A vision-based human digital twin modeling approach for adaptive human-robot collaboration. J. Manufact. Sci. Eng. **145**(12), 121002 (2023)
23. Fang, X., Xu, M., Xu, S., Zhao, P.: A deep learning framework for predicting cyber attacks rates. EURASIP J. Inform. Sec. **2019**, 5 (2019)
24. Fang, Z., Xu, M., Xu, S., Hu, T.: A framework for predicting data breach risk: leveraging dependence to cope with sparsity. IEEE T-IFS **16**, 2186–2201 (2021)
25. Ficke, E., Bateman, R., Xu, S.: Autocrat: automatic cumulative reconstruction of alert trees. In: Proceedings of International Conference on Science of Cyber Security (SciSec 2024), (2024)
26. Ficke, E., Xu, S.: APIN: automatic attack path identification in computer networks. In: IEEE International Conference on Intelligence and Security Informatics, ISI 2020, Arlington, VA, USA, 9-10 November 2020, pp. 1–6 (2020)
27. Han, Y., Lu, W., Xu, S.: Characterizing the power of moving target defense via cyber epidemic dynamics. In: HotSoS, pp. 1–12 (2014)
28. Han, Y., Lu, W., Xu, S.: Preventive and reactive cyber defense dynamics with ergodic time-dependent parameters is globally attractive. IEEE TNSE **8**(3), 2517–2532 (2021)
29. Harrison K., Xu, S.: Protecting cryptographic keys from memory disclosures. In: IEEE/IFIP DSN 2007, pp. 137–143 (2007)
30. He, S., et al.: Blockchain-based automated and robust cyber security management. J. Parallel Distributed Comput. **163**, 62–82 (2022)
31. Irshad, R.R., et al.: Iot-enabled secure and scalable cloud architecture for multi-user systems: a hybrid post-quantum cryptographic and blockchain based approach towards a trustworthy cloud computing. IEEE Access (2023)

32. Jho, N.-S., Hwang, J.Y., Cheon, J.H., Kim, M.-H., Lee, D.H., Yoo, E.S.: One-way chain based broadcast encryption schemes. In: Cramer, R. (ed.) EUROCRYPT 2005. LNCS, vol. 3494, pp. 559–574. Springer, Heidelberg (2005). https://doi.org/10.1007/11426639_33
33. Khandelwal, S.: Nearly half of the norway population exposed in healthcare data breach. In: The Hacker News, p. 1. The Hacker News (2018)
34. Li, S., Baiocco, A., Xu, S.: Characterizing privacy risks in healthcare iot systems. In: Abie, H., Gkioulos, V., Katsikas, S., Pirbhulal, S. (eds.) Secure and Resilient Digital Transformation of Healthcare. SUNRISE 2023. CCIS, vol. 1884. Springer, Cham (2024). https://doi.org/10.1007/978-3-031-55829-0_4
35. Li, Z., et al.: Robin: a novel method to produce robust interpreters for deep learning-based code classifiers. In: The 38th IEEE/ACM International Conference on Automated Software Engineering (ASE2023) (2023)
36. Li, Z., Zou, D., Xu, S., Jin, H., Qi, H., Hu, J.: Vulpecker: an automated vulnerability detection system based on code similarity analysis. In: Proceedings of ACSAC 2016, pp. 201–213 (2016)
37. Li, Z., Zou, D., Xu, S., Jin, H., Zhu, Y., Chen, Z.: Sysevr: a framework for using deep learning to detect software vulnerabilities. IEEE Trans. Dependable Sec. Comput. (2021)
38. Li, Z., et al.: Vuldeepecker: a deep learning-based system for vulnerability detection. In: Proceedings of NDSS 2018 (2018)
39. Longtchi, T., Rodriguez, R.M., Al-Shawaf, L., Atyabi, A., Shouhuai, X.: Internet-based social engineering psychology, attacks, and defenses: a survey. Proc. IEEE **112**(3), 210–246 (2024)
40. Longtchi, T., Xu, S.: Characterizing the evolution of psychological factors exploited by malicious emails. In: Proceedings of International Conference on Science of Cyber Security (SciSec 2024) (2024)
41. Longtchi, T., Xu, S.: Characterizing the evolution of psychological tactics and techniques exploited by malicious emails. In: Proceedings of International Conference on Science of Cyber Security (SciSec 2024) (2024)
42. Longtchi, T.T.: Quantifying psychological sophistication of malicious emails. IEEE Access (2024)
43. Loscocco, P., Smalley, S., Muckelbauer, P., Taylor, R., Turner, S., Farrell, J.: The inevitability of failure: The flawed assumption of security in modern computing environments. In: Proc. 21st National Information Systems Security Conference (NISSC 1998) (1998)
44. Lu, W., Xu, S., Yi, X.: Optimizing active cyber defense dynamics. In: Proceedings of GameSec 2013, pp. 206–225 (2013)
45. Lynch, N.: Distributed Algorithms. Morgan Kaufmann (1996)
46. Mireles, J., Ficke, E., Cho, J., Hurley, P., Xu, S.: Metrics towards measuring cyber agility. IEEE Trans. Inf. Forensics Secur. **14**(12), 3217–3232 (2019)
47. Moganedi, S., Dlamini, S.: Security by design: rethinking resilience of iot in healthcare. In: 2021 IST-Africa Conference (IST-Africa), pp. 1–9. IEEE (2021)
48. Montañez, R., et al.: Quantifying psychological sophistication of malicious emails. In: Proceedings of International Conference on Science of Cyber Security (SciSec 2023), pp. 319–331 (2023)
49. Rodriguez, R.M., Xu, S.: Cyber social engineering kill chain. In *Science of Cyber Security: 4th International Conference, SciSec 2022, Matsue, Japan, August 10–12, 2022, Revised Selected Papers*, pages 487–504. Springer, 2022
50. Montañez, R., Golob, E., Shouhuai, X.: Human cognition through the lens of social engineering cyberattacks. Front. Psychol. **11**, 1755 (2020)
51. Naor, D., Naor, M., Lotspiech, J.: Revocation and tracing schemes for stateless receivers. In: Kilian, J. (ed.) CRYPTO 2001. LNCS, vol. 2139, pp. 41–62. Springer, Heidelberg (2001). https://doi.org/10.1007/3-540-44647-8_3

52. Neisser, U.: Cognitive Psychology: Classic Edition (1st ed.). Psychology Press (2014)
53. Nguyen, T.N.: Cybonto: towards human cognitive digital twins for cybersecurity. arXiv preprint arXiv:2108.00551 (2021)
54. Nifakos, S., et al.: Influence of human factors on cyber security within healthcare organisations: a systematic review. Sensors **21**(15), 5119 (2021)
55. Obidallah, W.J.: Enhancing healthcare security measures in iott applications through a hesitant fuzzy-based integrated approach. AIMS Math **9**, 9020–9048 (2024)
56. Pendleton, M., Garcia-Lebron, R., Cho, J.-H., Xu, S.: A survey on systems security metrics. ACM Comput. Surv. **49**(4), 621–6235 (2016)
57. Peng, C., Maochao, X., Shouhuai, X., Taizhong, H.: Modeling and predicting extreme cyber attack rates via marked point processes. J. Appl. Stat. **44**(14), 2534–2563 (2017)
58. Pirbhulal, S., Abie, H., Shukla, A.: Towards a novel framework for reinforcing cybersecurity using digital twins in iot-based healthcare applications. In: 2022 IEEE 95th Vehicular Technology Conference:(VTC2022-Spring), pp. 1–5. IEEE (2022)
59. Pirbhulal, S., Abie, H., Shukla, A., Katt, B.: A cognitive digital twin architecture for cybersecurity in iot-based smart homes. In: Suryadevara, N.K., George, B., Jayasundera, K.P., Mukhopadhyay, S.C. (eds.) Sensing Technology. ICST 2022. LNEE, vol. 1035. Springer, Cham (2023). https://doi.org/10.1007/978-3-031-29871-4_8
60. Pirbhulal, S., Chockalingam, S., Abie, H., Lau, N.: Cognitive digital twins for improving security in IT-OT enabled healthcare applications. In: Moallem, A. (eds) HCI for Cybersecurity, Privacy and Trust. HCII 2024. LNCS, vol. 14729. Springer, Cham (2024). https://doi.org/10.1007/978-3-031-61382-1_10
61. Saeed, M.M.A., Saeed, R.A., Ahmed, Z.E.: Data security and privacy in the age of ai and digital twins. In: Digital Twin Technology and AI Implementations in Future-Focused Businesses, pp. 99–124. IGI Global (2024)
62. Sarp, S., Kuzlu, M., Zhao, Y., Gueler, O.: Digital twin in healthcare: a study for chronic wound management. IEEE J. Biomed. Health Inform. (2023)
63. Sun, Z., Xu, M., Schweitzer, K., Bateman, R., Kott, A., Xu, S.: Cyber attacks against enterprise networks: Characterization, modeling and forecasting. In: Proc. of SciSec 2023 (2023)
64. Tariq, N., Qamar, A., Asim, M., Khan, F.A.: Blockchain and smart healthcare security: a survey. Proc. Comput. Sci. **175**, 615–620 (2020)
65. Thamotharan, P., et al.: Human digital twin for personalized elderly type 2 diabetes management. J. Clin. Med. **12**(6), 2094 (2023)
66. Théron, P., Kott, A.: When autonomous intelligent goodware will fight autonomous intelligent malware: A possible future of cyber defense. In: IEEE MILCOM, pp. 1–7 (2019)
67. Turner, J., Li, S., Xu, S.: Jamming-resistant communications via cryptographic secret sharing. In: IEEE International Conference on Communications (2024)
68. Van Mieghem, P., Omic, J., Kooij, R.: Virus spread in networks. IEEE/ACM Trans. Netw. **17**(1), 1–14 (2008)
69. Wallner, D., Harder, E., Agee, R.: Key management for multicast: Issues and architectures. Internet Draft, Sept (1998)
70. Wang, Y., Chakrabarti, D., Wang, C., Faloutsos, C.: Epidemic spreading in real networks: an eigenvalue viewpoint. In: IEEE SRDS 2003, pp. 25–34 (2003)
71. Wong, C., Gouda, M., Lam, S.: Secure group communication using key graphs. IEEE/ACM Trans. Netw. (Preliminary version in SIGCOMM 1998) **8** (2000)
72. Xu, M., Da, G., Xu, S.: Cyber epidemic models with dependences. Internet Mathematics **11**(1), 62–92 (2015)
73. Xu, M., Hua, L., Xu, S.: A vine copula model for predicting the effectiveness of cyber defense early-warning. Technometrics **59**(4), 508–520 (2017)
74. Xu, M., Schweitzer, K.M., Bateman, R.M., Xu, S.: Modeling and predicting cyber hacking breaches. IEEE T-IFS **13**(11), 2856–2871 (2018)

75. Xu, M., Xu, S.: An extended stochastic model for quantitative security analysis of networked systems. Internet Mathematics **8**(3), 288–320 (2012)
76. Xu, S.: On the security of group communication schemes. J. Comput. Secur. **15**(1), 129–169 (2007)
77. Xu, S.: The cybersecurity dynamics way of thinking and landscape (invited paper). In: ACM Workshop on Moving Target Defense (2020)
78. Xu, S., Li, X., Parker, T., Wang, X.: Exploiting trust-based social networks for distributed protection of sensitive data. IEEE T-IFS **6**(1), 39–52 (2011)
79. Xu, S., Lu, W., Xu, L.: Push- and pull-based epidemic spreading in networks: thresholds and deeper insights. ACM TAAS **7**(3) (2012)
80. Xu, S., Lu, W., Xu, L., Zhan, Z.: Adaptive epidemic dynamics in networks: thresholds and control. ACM TAAS **8**(4) (2014)
81. Xu, S.: Cybersecurity dynamics. In: Proceedings of Symposium on the Science of Security (HotSoS 2014), pp. 14:1–14:2 (2014)
82. Xu, S.: Cybersecurity dynamics: a foundation for the science of cybersecurity. In: Proactive and Dynamic Network Defense, vol. 74, pp. 1–31. Springer (2019)
83. Xu, S: Sarr: a cybersecurity metrics and quantification framework. In: Third International Conference on Science of Cyber Security (SciSec 2021), pp. 3–17 (2021)
84. Shouhuai, X., Wenlian, L., Li, H.: A stochastic model of active cyber defense dynamics. Internet Mathematics **11**(1), 23–61 (2015)
85. Xu, S., Yung, M.: Expecting the unexpected: towards robust credential infrastructure. In: Dingledine, R., Golle, P. (eds.) FC 2009. LNCS, vol. 5628, pp. 201–221. Springer, Heidelberg (2009). https://doi.org/10.1007/978-3-642-03549-4_12
86. Yanamala, A.K.Y.: Data-driven and artificial intelligence (ai) approach for modelling and analyzing healthcare security practice: a systematic review. Revista de Inteligencia Artificial en Medicina **14**(1), 54–83 (2023)
87. Zhan, Z., Maochao, X., Shouhuai, X.: Characterizing honeypot-captured cyber attacks: statistical framework and case study. IEEE T-IFS **8**(11), 1775–1789 (2013)
88. Zhan, Z., Maochao, X., Shouhuai, X.: Predicting cyber attack rates with extreme values. IEEE Trans. Inf. Forensics Secur. **10**(8), 1666–1677 (2015)
89. Zheng, R., Lu, W., Xu, S.: Active cyber defense dynamics exhibiting rich phenomena. In: Proc. HotSoS (2015)
90. Zheng, R., Lu, W., Xu, S.: Preventive and reactive cyber defense dynamics is globally stable. IEEE TNSE **5**(2), 156–170 (2018)
91. Zou, D., Wang, S., Xu, S., Li, Z., Jin, H.: μvuldeepecker: a deep learning-based system for multiclass vulnerability detection. IEEE TDSC (2020)

Dynamic Safety and Security Risk Assessment in Healthcare and Critical Infrastructures

Sabarathinam Chockalingam[1](✉), Sandeep Pirbhulal[2], Pallavi Kaliyar[3], and Habtamu Abie[2]

[1] Institute for Energy Technology, Os Alle 5, 1777 Halden, Norway
Sabarathinam.Chockalingam@ife.no
[2] Norwegian Computing Center, Blindern, PO Box 114, 0314 Oslo, Norway
{sandeep,abie}@nr.no
[3] Norwegian University of Science and Technology, 2815 Gjøvik, Norway
Pallavi.Kaliyar@gmail.com

Abstract. Critical Infrastructures, such as healthcare, are essential for maintaining societal well-being and bolstering the nation's economy. The growing integration of Cyber Physical Systems (CPSs), such as social robots, into these infrastructures has made them more susceptible to both random faults and cyber-attacks. Traditional risk assessment frameworks typically address either safety or security risks, but often lack the capability to dynamically assess and mitigate both in an integrated manner. In our previous work, we developed a Bayesian Network (BN) framework that helps in developing BN models for distinguishing random faults and attacks, primarily for diagnostic purposes. However, this framework did not include proactive security measures. In this study, we enhance the BN framework to facilitate the development of models that incorporate proactive security measures by considering mitigating factors. In addition, we introduce extended Component Fault Trees (CFTs) for knowledge elicitation, leveraging their formal structure and practitioners' familiarity with Fault Tree analysis. We propose a translation scheme from extended CFTs to BNs to further refine the framework. The effectiveness of this framework is demonstrated through two use cases: remote patient monitoring in healthcare, and the deployment of social robots in smart cities. This study presents a holistic framework for dynamic safety and security risk assessment in critical environments, featuring a closed feedback loop between information sources and the risk evaluation and treatment stages to ensure continuous monitoring, analysis, and adaptation to evolving risks.

Keywords: Adaptive Security · Bayesian Network · Component Fault Tree · Graph-based modeling · Healthcare · Risk assessment · Safety · Smart Cities · Social Robots

1 Introduction

1.1 Overview

Critical Infrastructures (CIs) are essential for maintaining a country's societal well-being and economic stability. Common CI sectors across nations include banking, digital infrastructure, drinking water, energy, financial market infrastructure, food (production, processing, and distribution), healthcare, public administration, space, transport, and wastewater [50]. The use of Cyber Physical Systems (CPS) like social robots in CIs has increased over the recent years, which has various benefits like improving the operational efficiency of CIs [45]. In addition, Operational Technology (OT) components, which manage and control physical devices in CIs, have also been increasing. However, this also introduces additional vulnerabilities to potential cyber-attacks and expands the attack surface in CIs [45]. Ukraine's power grid attack in addition Triton malware attack on a petrochemical plant in Saudi Arabia are typical examples of cyber-attacks on the OT environment [46, 47].

Risk management is critical in dealing with both intentional (security-related) and unintentional (safety-related) threats [48]. Risk assessment is an important phase of the risk management process because it serves as the foundation for risk treatment decisions. Chockalingam et al. identified seven different integrated safety and security risk assessment methods in the scientific literature [41]. Furthermore, they analyzed the identified methods using five different comparison criteria like steps involved, stage(s) of risk assessment process addressed. Based on the analysis, they highlighted that the identified integrated safety and security risk assessment methods do not incorporate real-time system information for dynamic risk assessment.

To address this gap, in our previous work, Chockalingam et al. developed a Bayesian Network (BN) framework that helps to develop models for distinguishing attacks and technical failures [24]. BNs provide a probabilistic framework for dynamic risk assessment, allowing the continuous updating of failure probabilities as new evidence is observed. However, the BN framework was primarily focused on diagnosis and lacked proactive security, limiting its ability to anticipate and prevent potential threats. Specifically, they lack a mechanism for evaluating the impact of preventive countermeasures and mitigation strategies in real time, which is essential for adapting to evolving threats. Furthermore, BNs pose challenges in knowledge elicitation. For instance, using BNs for knowledge elicitation with domain experts can be challenging, as it is often time-consuming to explain the concept of BNs and make immediate adjustments to their structure during discussions in expert knowledge elicitation sessions. However, Component Fault Trees (CFTs) provide a structured, hierarchical representation of system failures, making it easier to identify the relationship between component-level issues and overall system vulnerabilities. In this study, we integrate BNs with CFTs, leveraging the strengths of both approaches. By combining the probabilistic reasoning of BNs with the structured, intuitive representation of CFTs, we enhance knowledge elicitation and enable dynamic risk assessment. In this study, we focus on knowledge-based BNs. To that end, this research aims to tackle the above-mentioned challenges by addressing the research question: *"How can an integrated framework that combines Bayesian Networks (BNs), and Component Fault Trees (CFTs) facilitate knowledge elicitation to develop BN models for proactive security, while dynamically distinguishing between intentional attacks and accidental technical failures?"*. The Research Objectives (ROs) are:

RO1. To extend the Bayesian Network (BN) framework for proactive security, enabling the development of BN models that distinguish between intentional attacks and accidental technical failures.

RO2. To develop an integrated process flow that combines Component Fault Trees (CFTs) and Bayesian Networks (BNs) to facilitate knowledge elicitation and enhance dynamic safety and security risk assessment.

RO3. To demonstrate the usefulness of the proposed framework using realistic use case scenarios.

1.2 Our Contributions

The main contributions of this paper are as follows:

- Extended BN framework to support proactive security that supports developing knowledge-based BN models for determining whether an abnormal behavior stems from an intentional attack or an accidental technical failure.
- Developed an integrated process flow that combines BNs and CFTs, facilitating efficient knowledge elicitation and enhancing dynamic safety and security risk assessments.
- Demonstrated our proposed approach using two use case scenarios: remote patient monitoring in healthcare and the use of social robots in smart cities.

The remainder of this paper is structured as follows: Sect. 2 provides an essential foundation on CFTs and BNs, along with an overview of safety and security challenges in healthcare and the use of social robots in smart cities. Section 3 reviews related work. In Sect. 4, we describe the proposed approach, followed by a description and demonstration of the use case scenarios. Section 5 discusses conclusions and future research directions.

2 Background

2.1 Component Fault Trees

A Fault Tree (FT) is a Directed Acyclic Graph (DAG) composed of two primary elements: events and gates [1]. An event represents an occurrence within the system and can be categorized as a top event, intermediate event, or basic event [2]. However, the key difference between a traditional FT and Component Fault Tree (CFT) lies in their focus. While FTs provide a broad analysis of system failures, considering both internal and external factors, CFTs provide more detailed, component-centric analysis of failures within a system [1, 3].

In a CFT, the top event is the primary failure or issue being analyzed in a system, typically resulting from component-level faults. Intermediate events occur because of one or more basic events and lead to the top event. For instance, in a hospital safety context, the top event can be *"Fire alarm fails to activate"*. Intermediate events leading to this could be *"power supply failure"*, *"smoke detector malfunction"*, and *"backup battery failure"*, all contributing to the top event. In this case, an OR gate would be used, as the occurrence of any of these events would trigger the top event. In this scenario, we focused on three different components within the fire alarm system: power supply, smoke detector, and backup battery within a fire alarm system. Each intermediate event is linked to specific basic events. For instance, *"power supply failure"* could be caused by *"wiring fault"*, while *"smoke detector malfunction"* could be caused by a *"detector not calibrated"*, or a *"dusty/blocked sensor"*, and *"backup battery failure"* could be caused by *"battery not charged"*. There are various advantages of CFTs over traditional FTs [1, 4, 5]:

- CFTs are modular, meaning that individual components or subsystems can be modeled separately and then integrated into a larger system model.
- Modularity allows for the reuse of CFTs across different projects or systems, saving time and effort in analyzing systems with common components.
- Traditional FTs are typically constructed for an entire system, and any changes to the system require the entire tree to be rebuilt. This makes traditional FTs less flexible and less reusable.

In essence, CFTs provide better scalability, easier maintenance, and more straightforward updates, while emphasizing component-centric analysis. However, CFTs do not inherently address security concerns. There have been efforts to integrate traditional FTs/CFTs with Attack Trees (ATs), which are specifically designed for security analysis [6–8]. Key advantages of combining FTs/CFTs with ATs are [6–8]:

- It supports holistic analysis of both safety and security.
- It improves the prioritization of risks.
- It helps in optimizing countermeasures especially by considering mutual reinforcement (i.e., measures that enhance both safety and security) and antagonism (i.e., when safety measures weaken security and vice-versa).
- It facilitates better communication among stakeholders.

2.2 Bayesian Networks

BNs are probabilistic models that include both a qualitative component (i.e., a DAG) and a quantitative component (conditional probabilities). BNs can be developed using expert knowledge, empirical data, or a combination of both. In this study, we focus on knowledge-based BNs. BNs are used to represent the communication within complex systems through dependencies and hierarchical structures [9]. Kumarasamy et al. applied BNs for detecting frauds in healthcare, demonstrating that the BNs are effective in exploiting the relational structure of attributes and provide better interpretability compared to other AI/ML approaches. Experimental results show that BNs outperforms random forest and logistic regression approaches in terms of F1 score for detecting fraudulent medical claims in real-life insurance scenarios. In [10], Pirbhulal et al. conducted a comprehensive study on graph theory and BNs, focusing on the integration of safety and security for risk assessment in different sectors such as healthcare, transportation, and smart grids. This study highlighted the importance of simultaneously ensuring both safety and security, as BNs effectively address uncertainty and incompleteness. Given the interdependence between safety and security, it is crucial to perform root cause analysis, and assess system performance using sensitivity analysis, statistical analysis, and expert evaluation.

2.3 Safety and Security Challenges in Healthcare

Modern healthcare systems face a range of security and privacy concerns as medical devices are connected to other healthcare systems, Internet of Things (IoT) networks, emergency and nursing stations, and cloud infrastructures. This interconnectedness creates multiple entry points for attackers, increasing the risk of both passive and active security threats [11]. As highlighted in [12], some of the major security threats for healthcare and other critical sectors include malware, ransomware, cyber espionage, Distributed Denial of Service (DDoS) attacks, phishing, insider threat, social engineering attacks, and identity theft. Ness et al. reported that, healthcare being highly sensitive, requires dynamic strategies to predict/identify, prevent, and evaluate security risks. In fact, at least 20% of medical device manufacturers have experienced ransomware or malware attacks in the last two years [12].

In addition to identifying security incidents, healthcare organizations must implement risk management processes to ensure a satisfactory level of safety for patients, medical staff, and infrastructure [13]. Key safety challenges in healthcare from a safety point of view are medication errors, patient falls, and chemical hazards. Therefore, there is a clear need for an integrated safety and security risk assessment approach in the healthcare sector to foster a safe and secure environment for both patients and medical service providers.

2.4 Safety and Security Challenges in the Use of Social Robots in Smart Cities

Social robots have various applications in smart cities [14, 15]. For instance, during the Covid-19 pandemic in Italy, a robot was used to assist doctors in remotely monitoring patients [16]. Similarly, in Budapest, a social robot supported medical staff by interacting with patients through a questionnaire to help those identified with coronavirus [16]. Furthermore, as a part of our ongoing SecuRoPS project [17], we aim to implement a social robot *ARI* in Fredrikstad municipality. In our project, as a part of a study, *ARI* provides services such as providing personalized recommendations on local attractions and current events in the city, while ensuring safety, security, and privacy. SecuRoPS and *ARI* will be further detailed in Sect. 3.

As social robots interact directly with people, it is essential to understand and address the safety and security challenges involved in their integration into cities in a sustainable manner. We outline several security-related threats to social robots:

- Threat actors may physically tamper with or abuse social robots in public spaces due to lack of continuous supervision. For instance, they could obstruct the robot's path, cover its sensors (such as cameras) with tapes, vandalize its components, or even steal the entire robot [18].
- Threat actors may replace legitimate files with malicious versions while interacting with social robots. For instance, when accessing a PDF file, they could execute malicious code or use drive-by-download methods to compromise the system [18, 19].
- Data transmitted between social robots in public spaces and central servers can be intercepted or manipulated, resulting in breaches [20].

In addition to security-related threats, safety is also equally important when deploying social robots in public places. It is essential to develop risk assessment methods that address both safety and security in an integrated manner, rather than treating them as separate issues.

3 Related Work

3.1 Safety and Security Risk Assessment

Risk analysis plays a significant role in dealing with both safety and security threats. In recent years, researchers from both industry and academia have increasingly focused on safety and security risk management [41]. Tai-hua et al. [42] developed a public security and safety risk assessment approach using fuzzy logic and BNs. In their research, the Dempster–Shafer evidence theory is applied to develop a synthesis algorithm based on matrix and weight analysis. However, a major limitation of this work is that it is tailored specifically for Chinese enterprises, requiring significant adjustments for other use cases.

Chao et al. [43] developed a consequence-based method, including a Dynamic Vulnerability Assessment Graph (DVAG) model for incorporating safety and security resources to decrease the risk of intentional attacks. The DVAG model is based on dynamic graphs, and takes into account safety barriers, security measures, and emergency responses. The method evaluates the potential consequences and probabilities of intentional attacks, allowing for the efficient allocation of safety and security measures. Cavalheiro et al. [44] presented an application for risk assessment and mitigation in ventricular enabled devices (VAD) using BN and Game Theory. Their work proposes a hierarchical supervisory control system that can dynamically, automatically, and securely manage VAD operation. The methodology is based on BN for patients' diagnoses, with Petri nets generating a VAD control algorithm and Safety Instrumented Systems ensuring system security. Although the study provides an approach for a better quality of life and more prolonged survival of patients, it does not specify potential threat actors.

Sabaliauskaite et al. developed an approach for aligning safety and security in CPS during the early development phases by synchronizing the safety and security lifecycles, based on the ISA84 and ISA99 standards [21]. This alignment is achieved by merging the safety and security lifecycle phases and introducing a unified model called Failure-Attack-Countermeasure (FACT) graph. The FACT graph combines safety artifacts including FTs and safety countermeasures with security artifacts including ATs and security countermeasures. However, this approach lacks dynamism and a feedback loop, making it less applicable during the operational phase. Fovino et al. introduced a novel approach for quantitative security risk assessment, combining traditional FTs with ATs. This combined approach enables the analysis of how malicious acts lead to system failures [22]. However, this approach does not focus on component-specific analysis. Similarly, Steiner et al. extended CFTs by incorporating ATs to model potential attacks that could lead to system failures [23]. However, their work is not applied to healthcare or using social robots in smart cities, nor is it used to develop BNs for analyzing root causes of abnormal behavior, which is the focus of our current study. In addition, the translation from CFT to BN formalism is missing, and also proactive security is lacking in their approach.

Chockalingam et al. proposed a BN framework including three different types of variables: contributory factors, the problem (which includes two states: accidental technical failure and intentional attack), and observations (or test results) as shown in Fig. 1 [24]. The main drawback of their framework is that mitigation measures for safety and security at the initial level are not considered. This could influence contributory factors. For instance, regular patching could reduce device vulnerability.

In addition to aiding in knowledge elicitation, extended fishbone diagrams were utilized during discussions with experts, which were subsequently translated in BN formalism for analysis [24]. However, extended fishbone diagrams lack formalism and are primarily qualitative, and may not sufficiently capture probability dependencies.

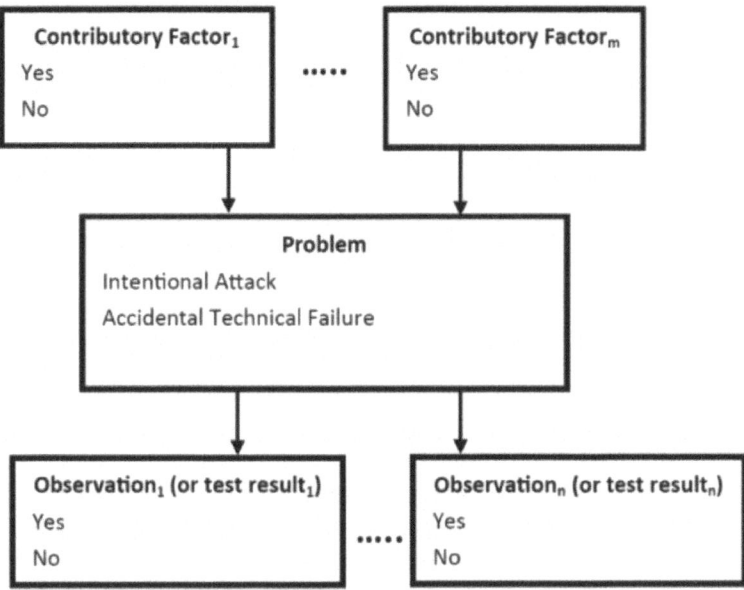

Fig. 1. BN Framework for Distinguishing Attacks and Technical Failures [24]

Significant efforts have been made in integrating safety and security risk assessment through various modeling techniques such as the use of FTs and ATs. However, approaches like the FACT graph are static and cannot be applied in the operational phase. Furthermore, although there have been attempts to combine CFT with AT, these approaches have not been used for root cause analysis or knowledge elicitation. Finally, our previous work utilized fishbone diagrams for knowledge elicitation. However, it lacks formalism, which CFTs can provide. Furthermore, there is a lack of CFT to BN formalism translation. These are the gaps that this current study would address and build on the related work.

3.2 Risk Assessment in Healthcare and Smart Cities

In the study [25], Shanmugam et al. presented various risk assessment approaches including TARA, NIST, ISO 27001, and IEEE (P2413) among others. They also highlighted the importance of novel and dynamic methodologies to address risks arising from varying conditions. Given the continuous challenges of security and privacy risks in medical devices, a risk assessment framework was developed to identify and modify potential risks, recommending mitigation measures. In [26], the authors highlighted the challenges of risk assessment in healthcare due to heterogeneity of devices with varying protocols, vulnerabilities, environments and functionalities. To address these challenges, hybrid fuzzy logic and Fuzzy Analytical Hierarchy Process was proposed to evaluate risks, offering effective solutions to different critical sectors. In their study, a case analysis was conducted for three medical devices - smartwatches, oximeters, and smart peak flow meters. A bluetooth attack was simulated to find potential vulnerabilities. The proposed approach calculated the risk level for each device, with smartwatches showing a risk level of 8.57 for injection attacks.

In [27], a risk-based adaptive authentication mechanism for continuous monitoring of dynamic characteristics in healthcare environments, using the naive Bayes algorithm to identify risks. A unique characteristic of their study was the adaptation process tailored to each phase. In [28], Sodhro et al. developed a lightweight approach for detecting failures in IoT based applications by integrating homomorphism encryption with workload assignment and transient fault awareness for addressing threats and failures. Healthcare risks may occur and be addressed differently compared to other critical sectors such as energy, transportation, and industry 4.0. The processing of sensitive information in healthcare and its exposure to attackers, can cause serious harm and directly impact individuals' lives. For instance, in September 2020, a ransomware attack on a German hospital led to the death of a 78-year-old female patient [29]. This attack disrupted the hospital's network, causing unnecessary rerouting of a critically ill patient, who died before reaching for treatment. Consequently, healthcare security and privacy protocols differ from those in other critical sectors such as the Health Insurance Portability and Accountability Act (HIPAA) in the USA [30], and General Data Protection Regulation (GDPR) in Europe [31].

Smart cities use advanced technologies like IoT and AI to improve urban living, efficient resource management and optimized services. However, these advancements also introduce significant safety and security risks due to increased connectivity. Efforts have been made to propose safety and/or security risk assessment methods in this context. González-Villa et al. developed a Decision Support System (DSS) that incorporates three layers: threat analysis, pedestrian movement simulation, and traffic monitoring [32]. This comprehensive DSS aims to support private operators, law enforcement agencies, and local authorities in effectively protecting vulnerable city targets. This is predominantly focused on physical security and safety. However, it lacks the consideration of cyber security risks and does not address the integration of social robots. Li et al. highlighted the role of intelligent traffic lights as key components for reducing road congestion and vehicle emissions in smart cities [33]. Furthermore, they also proposed a bi-level game theoretic framework for assessing cyber security risks in these traffic light systems.

However, this approach does not address safety and cyber security risks in an integrated manner.

In smart cities, social robots are also increasingly deployed to assist in various tasks, such as public service, healthcare and elderly care. This is mainly to enhance and personalize such services. However, the integration of social robots also brings in new safety and security risks in addition to privacy risks, as they interact with people directly in dynamic environments. Prabhu et al. analyzed security and privacy risks corresponding to the use of social robots in environments where personal interactions and data handling are prevalent [34]. However, their study lacks an assessment of safety risks and does not incorporate a dynamic approach to risk assessment. Denning et al. conducted an experimental analysis to identify security and privacy issues in three different household robots including WowWee Rovio, Erector Spykee, and WowWee RoboSapien V2 [35]. Based on their findings, they proposed a set of design questions aimed at guiding the development of household robots that prioritize security and user privacy. However, this approach does not provide a dynamic approach for assessing safety and security risks. In our previous work, Ayele et al. identified and analyzed potential threat actors targeting social robots in public spaces, the methods of attack that they might employ and the vulnerabilities that these robots possess [36]. Furthermore, Oruma et al. conducted a systematic mapping study to review and analyze existing literature on social robots with a focus on various security aspects [37]. This includes physical safety, data privacy, cyber security, and legal/ethical considerations.

Based on the related work, the focus has been primarily on identifying security and privacy risks. However, there is a lack of comprehensive risk assessment methods for social robots that integrate and address both safety and security risk jointly. Furthermore, the existing stand-alone security risk assessment methods lack a dynamic and adaptive approach.

3.3 Social Robots in the Context of Smart Cities and Healthcare

As a part of our ongoing SecuRoPS project, we are developing a user-centered framework to address cyber security challenges associated with social robots in public spaces. This framework includes a structured process, threat models, design principles, and guidelines aimed at ensuring the safety, security and privacy of citizens interacting with these systems. In addition, it provides reusable models and components that can be used by robot developers, owners, and other stakeholders to build secure robots and effectively monitor and respond to security incidents. ARI robot from PAL robotics is used as a part of the SecuRoPS project in our studies as shown in Fig. 2.

Cooper et al. conducted a review on the challenges faced by older adults, individuals with limited mobility, hospital patients, isolated healthcare users, and how socially assistive robots can be employed to support them [38]. Ragno et al. performed a review on the use of social robots in healthcare, focusing on their characteristics, technical requirements, and solutions [39]. This study highlights the applications of social robots in environments such as nursing homes, hospitals, and private homes, where they assist elderly, individuals with disabilities, children, and medical staff. González-González et al. conducted a systematic review on the current social robot design and their interactions with patients [40]. Their findings revealed that many of these initiatives and projects

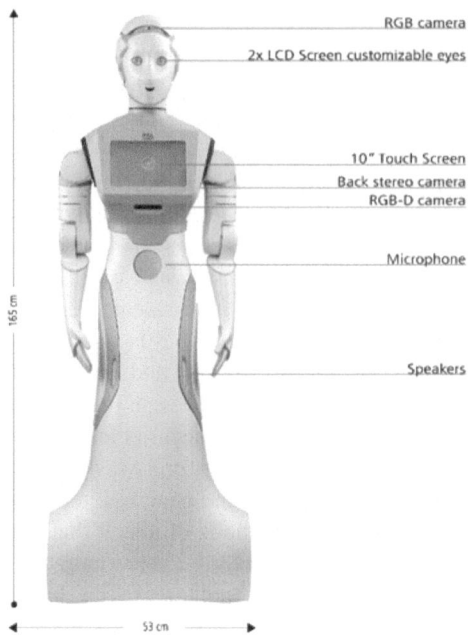

Fig. 2. ARI's Components (c) PAL Robotics [36]

involving social robots are targeted toward supporting elderly individuals and children, particularly in managing conditions such as dementia, autism spectrum disorder, cancer, and diabetes.

As shown in Fig. 2., social robots consist of different technical components, which are susceptible to both technical failures and cyber-attacks. For instance, an ARI robot's motor system responsible for controlling limb movement could experience a mechanical failure. This could lead to an inability of ARI robots to perform physical tasks such as waving or picking up objects. On the other hand, an adversary could infiltrate the ARI robot's control software by injecting malicious code. This code could target the motor control system, sending false signals to the motor responsible for limb movement. As a result, the robot might experience abnormal or non-functional limb movements, mimicking the symptoms of a mechanical failure. In that case, there is a need for dynamic and adaptive risk assessment methods that integrate both safety and security to have an holistic view, which is currently lackin

4 Proposed Security and Safety Risk Assessment Approach

This section outlines our proposed approach, detailing the process flow, the extended BN framework, the holistic framework for dynamic safety and security risk assessment, and the translation of CFTs to BNs.

Our proposed approach for dynamic safety and security risk assessment is structured to support continuous learning and adaptation. Figure 3 illustrates the main components of this process.

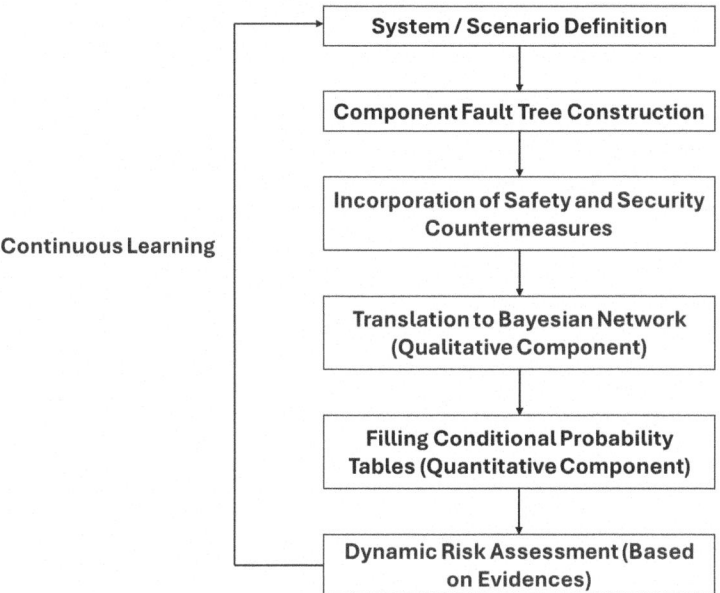

Fig. 3. Process Flow for our Dynamic Safety and Security Risk Assessment

- **System/Scenario Definition Phase:** In this phase, the system is thoroughly analyzed to identify key components and potential abnormal behavior scenarios at both system and component levels.
- **Development of CFTs:** Based on this analysis, CFTs are developed through knowledge elicitation with experts. Building on previous work [23], we combine CFTs with ATs to take into account contributory factors related to both technical failures and potential attacks that could lead to system or component failures. In addition, safety and security mitigation measures are incorporated at the basic event level in the CFT. This integration supports proactive security by mitigating potential system and component failures based on the initial system design and insights gained through continuous learning, which is a novel aspect of our proposed approach.
- **Translation of CFTs into BNs:** The next step involves translating the developed CFT into a qualitative BN using our proposed translation scheme. This aligns with our extended BN framework, as shown in Fig. 4.

Our Proposed Translation Scheme from CFTs to BNs: (i) Each basic event in the CFT is represented as a contributory factor node in the BN. (ii) OR gates in the CFT are translated into probabilistic dependencies in the BN. This means that if any contributory factor is true, it increases the probability of a failure at the system level. (iii) AND gates are similarly translated into probabilistic dependencies, where all events need to occur for the failure to happen. (iv) Mitigation measures in the CFT map directly to corresponding mitigation measures in the BN. Each mitigating measure is a parent node to its related contributory factors. (v) The top event of the CFT is translated into the problem node in the BN, with states representing either intentional attack or technical failure.

- **Populating the BN with Data:** This translated BN will be populated with observations and conditional probabilities based on expert knowledge and/or empirical data. However, this step falls outside of the scope of this study.
- **Dynamic Risk Assessment:** Finally, the developed BN model will be applied for dynamic risk assessment by incorporating known evidence to determine posterior probabilities. This process helps in identifying potential root causes based on the evidence provided by operators.

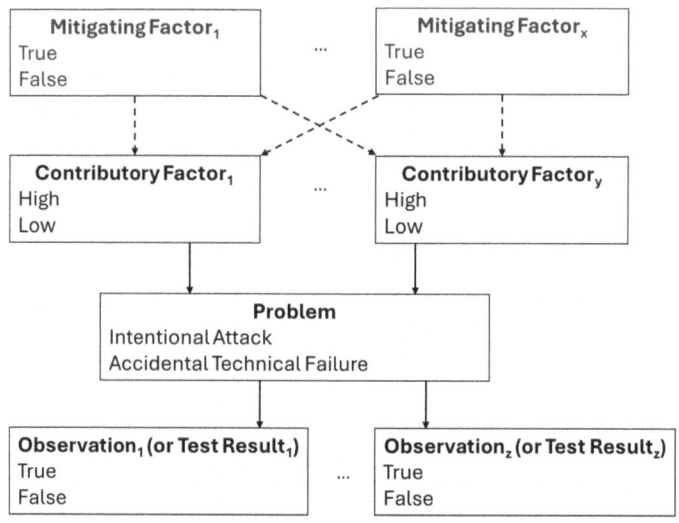

Fig. 4. Extended BN Framework

Based on the related work, Chockalingam et al. developed a three-level BN including contributory factors, the problem, and observations (or test results) [24]. While this approach is useful for diagnosing problems after they occur, it does not sufficiently address the preventive measures that can reduce the likelihood of contributory factors or the problem occurring in the first place. By extending this BN framework, we can include proactive components, such as safety and security countermeasures that enhance the system's resilience against both failures and attacks. Without these mitigating factors, the BN model based on our initial framework focuses solely on problem identification after occurrence, rather than on reducing the probability of occurrence. BN models developed using our extended BN framework will help in both proactive and reactive safety and security.

Figure 5 presents a holistic framework for dynamic safety and security risk assessment, aimed at analyzing, evaluating, and mitigating intentional and unintentional risks. This framework includes four main stages:

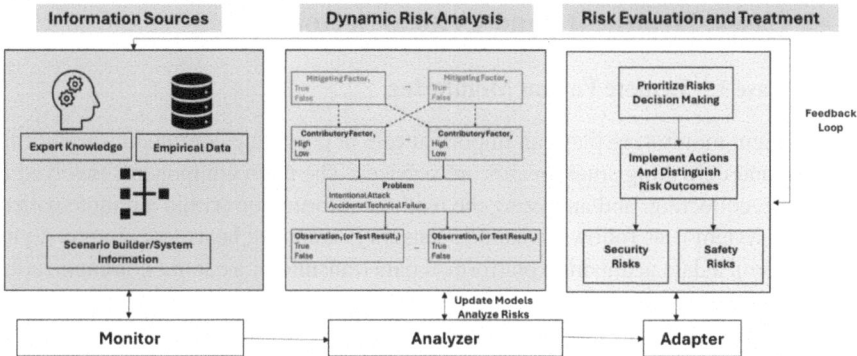

Fig. 5. Holistic Framework for Dynamic Safety and Security Risk Assessment

Information Sources: To develop a holistic approach, it is important to gather information from heterogeneous sources such as expert knowledge, empirical data. Expert knowledge provides valuable insights into safety and security risks in healthcare and other critical sectors, leveraging contextual and domain knowledge. Empirical data, on the other hand, plays a key role by providing critical information based on simulations and/or real-world experiments, which supplements contextual and domain knowledge.

Dynamic Risk Analysis: This stage outlines the necessary steps for dynamic risk assessment from both safety (technical failures) and security (attacks) perspectives, as elaborated in Fig. 4. Inputs from information sources are used to conduct root cause analysis of risks, whether caused by intentional attacks or accidental technical failures. This process enables a holistic view of potential safety and security risks and serves as the foundation for putting in place mitigation measures.

Risk Evaluation and Treatment: This stage is important for the development of a comprehensive protection framework. First, we perform risk evaluation to understand the significance of identified risks and prioritize them for treatment. Once the risks are evaluated, mitigation measures are implemented to respond to or prevent both safety and security risks taking into account mutual reinforcement and antagonism. Mutual reinforcement occurs when safety and security measures complement each other, strengthening overall system resilience against risks [51]. Antagonism arises when safety and security measures conflict, potentially diminishing each other's effectiveness in risk mitigation [52].

Adaptive Dynamics: A closed feedback loop is established between the information sources and the risk evaluation and treatment stages. As new data sources are identified, conditions for data collection and risk assessment are automatically updated. This feedback loop provides updated mitigation measures for the considered system, ensuring continuous monitoring, analysis, and adaptation to the evolving safety and security risks.

5 Use Cases: Healthcare and Critical Sectors

5.1 Use Case 1 – Remote Patient Monitoring

Remote patient monitoring plays an important role in providing continuous monitoring of patients and delivering smart healthcare services. The main components involved in transmitting, collecting, and analyzing the medical information within a remote patient monitoring system is as follows: wearable sensors (Examples: heart rate monitors, glucose monitors), a data acquisition platform, a data transmitter, a central communication hub, cloud processing (for storage, analytics, and visualization), and healthcare provider interfaces [49].

Based on the system components, we developed a CFT for the top event, defined as *"Remote Patient Monitoring System Failure"*. We identified four main components including: wearable sensors, the data acquisition platform, the data transmitter, and the central communication hub. A failure in any of these components could independently lead to the top event. For each component, we outlined failure causes and attack vectors as basic events, identifying factors that could contribute to system failure. For instance, *"battery depletion"* or *"sensor spoofing"* can lead to *"wearable sensor failure"*, impacting the remote patient monitoring system's functionality. To enhance system resilience, we incorporated specific mitigation measures as shown in Fig. 6. For example, *"real-time battery monitoring"* serves as a preventive safety measure to address potential failure caused by *"battery depletion"*, while *"using cryptographic authentication technique"* serves as a preventive security measure to mitigate the security risk posed by *"sensor spoofing"*. These contributory factors and mitigating factors can be identified through knowledge elicitation with experts. This will then be translated into a BN based on our translation scheme.

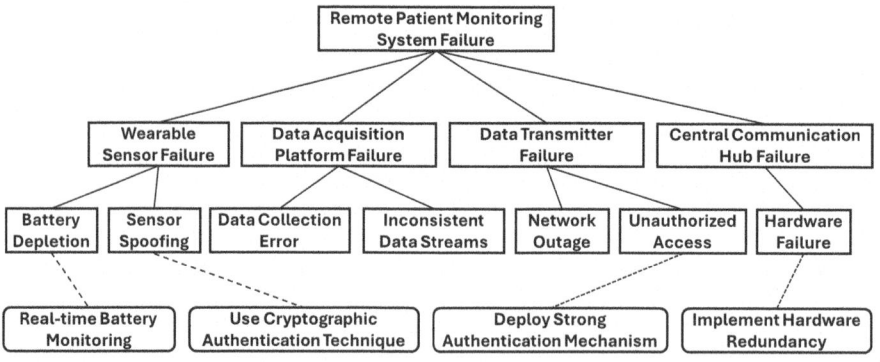

Fig. 6. CFT based on our Proposed Approach – Use Case: Example (Remote Patient Monitoring)

CFTs provides a component-centric view of failures and potential attacks that may lead to broader system weaknesses, enabling root cause analysis at the component level. However, CFTs are inherently static and only support forward reasoning. In Fig. 7, we illustrate the translation of CFTs into BNs using our proposed translation scheme, providing a dynamic solution that enables probabilistic analysis with structured visualization and conditional probabilities. For instance, by providing evidence for certain contributory factors and mitigation measures, the BN dynamically calculates the posterior probabilities of other nodes, including the problem node. This calculation helps identify which root cause is most likely, offering a clear indication of where intervention may be needed.

The example BN model, based on Fig. 6 and illustrated in Fig. 7, identifies key contributory factors, such as *"Battery Depletion"* and *"Sensor Spoofing"*, which could lead to a *"Wearable Sensor Failure"*. The *"Real-time Battery Monitoring"* and *"Cryptographic Authentication"* nodes act as mitigation measures, reducing the likelihood of battery depletion and spoofing, respectively. If battery depletion or sensor spoofing occurs, they increase the probability of wearable sensor failure, categorized here as either a fault (safety issue) or an attack (security issue). A failure at the sensor level could result in observable effects, like a *"Sudden Change of Wearable Sensor Measurements"*. By observing these symptoms and inputting evidence about contributory factors, the BN can calculate posterior probabilities, indicating the most probable root cause of a wearable sensor failure. This model allows for a dynamic assessment of risks, supporting both preventive measures and real-time diagnosis.

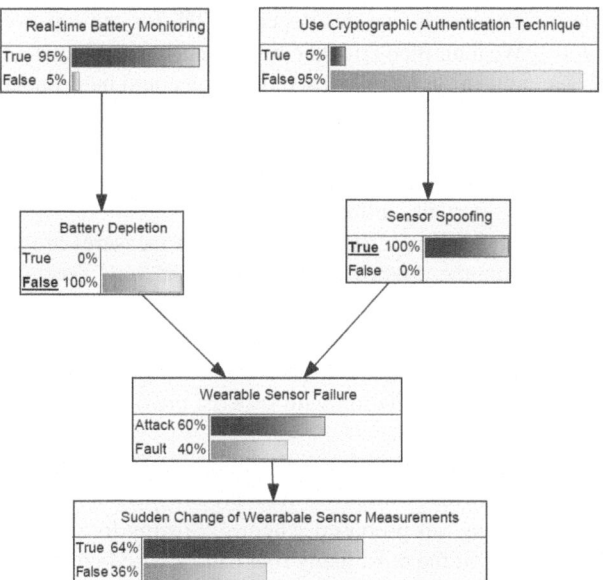

Fig. 7. BN – Use Case: Example (Remote Patient Monitoring)

5.2 Use Case 2 – Smart Cities (Social Robots)

Social robots are increasingly integrated into smart cities. The main components of ARI robot is as follows: sensors (for vision and object detection: realSense D435i RGB-D), communication module, range finder (YDLIDAR TG15), Natural Language Processing (NLP) unit (Intel i5/i7/i9 processors paired with Nvidia Xavier NX or Orin GPUs for AI processing), battery (24V/40Ah battery (upgradable to 60Ah) and provides an operational autonomy of 8–12 h).

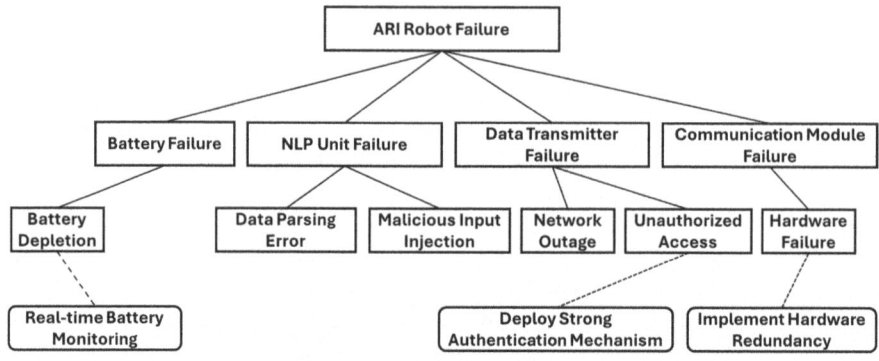

Fig. 8. CFT – Use Case: Example (Social Robots)

Based on these components, we developed a CFT for the top event, defined as *"ARI Robot Failure"*. We identified critical components such as battery, NLP unit, data transmitter, and communication module, each of which could independently lead to the top event if a failure occurs. For each component, we outlined potential contributory factors as basic events, identifying factors that could contribute to system failure. For example, *"battery depletion"* can result in an *"ARI Robot Failure,"* affecting the robot's functionality within the smart city infrastructure.

To strengthen system resilience, specific mitigation measures are incorporated, as shown in Fig. 8. For instance, *"real-time battery monitoring"* serves as a preventive safety measure to address potential failures due to battery depletion, while *"deploying strong authentication mechanisms"* acts as a security measure to mitigate risks associated with communication interference. Typically, these contributory and mitigation factors are identified through knowledge elicitation with experts, providing a structured approach to defining potential vulnerabilities.

The CFT offers a component-centric view of failures and potential attacks, enabling root cause analysis at the component level. To overcome the static nature of CFTs, we translated it into a BN using our proposed scheme, allowing for dynamic probabilistic analysis and identification of the most likely root causes based on entered evidence.

The example BN model, based on Fig. 8 and illustrated in Fig. 9, identifies key contributory factors, such as *"Battery Failure"* and *"Data Transmitter Failure,"* which could lead to *"ARI Robot Failure"*. Mitigation measures, like *"Real-time Battery Monitoring"* and *"Deploying Strong Authentication,"* reduce the likelihood of these failures. If battery depletion or data transmitter failure occurs, they increase the probability of ARI Robot Failure, classified here as either a fault (safety issue) or an attack (security issue). A failure at the robot level could lead to observable impacts, such as *"Redundant Battery Working"*. By observing these symptoms and inputting evidence related to contributory factors and mitigating factors, the BN calculates posterior probabilities, highlighting the most likely root cause of the ARI Robot Failure.

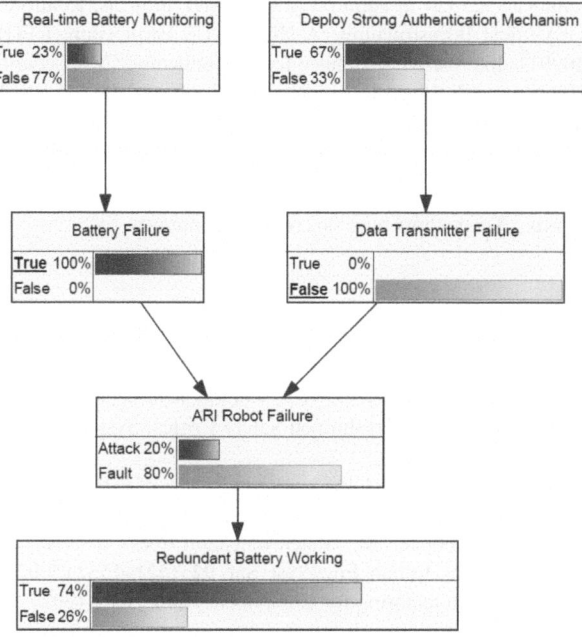

Fig. 9. BN– Use Case: Example (Social Robots)

6 Conclusions and Future Work Directions

This study addresses the critical need for a holistic framework to support developing models that dynamically assess and mitigate both safety and security risks in CIs, particularly in the context of healthcare and smart cities. In addition, the developed holistic framework includes a closed feedback loop between different stages to learn continuously and adaptively. By extending the BN framework and integrating it with CFTs, we provide a novel approach to develop models that identify and distinguish attacks and random faults. This integrated framework leverages the strengths of both BNs and CFTs, providing a structured and probabilistic method for dynamic risk assessment and enabling the continuous updating of risk profiles based on new evidence. The framework's usefulness has been demonstrated through two use cases: remote patient monitoring in healthcare and deployment of social robots in smart cities. Our study makes three key contributions: an extended BN framework that not only diagnoses but also incorporates proactive security by considering mitigating factors, a process flow integrating CFTs and BNs for knowledge elicitation and dynamic risk assessment, demonstration of the usefulness in healthcare and smart city use cases. In the future, the proposed framework and the translated scheme would be evaluated in a realistic setting. Furthermore, the applicability of the proposed framework in other domains should be explored.

Acknowledgments. This research is funded from the Research Council of Norway through, the SFI Norwegian Centre for Cybersecurity in Critical Sectors (NORCICS), with the project number #310105 and User-centred Security Framework for Social Robots in Public Space (SecuRoPS), with the project number #321324 in addition to INTPART projects, Reinforcing Competence in Cybersecurity of Critical Infrastructures: A Norway-US Partnership (RECYCIN), with the project number #309911, International Alliance for Strengthening Cybersecurity and Privacy in Healthcare (CybAlliance), with the project number #337316, and the EU ENFIELD (European Lighthouse To Manifest Trustworthy and Green AI) project received funding from the European Union's HORIZON Research and Innovation Programme under the grant agreement No 101120657.

Disclosure of Interests. The authors have no competing interests.

References

1. Kaiser, B., Liggesmeyer, P., Mäckel, O.: A new component concept for fault trees. In: Proceedings of the 8th Australian Workshop on Safety Critical Systems and Software, vol. 33, pp. 37–46 (2003)
2. Phan, H.T.: An incremental approach to identifying causes of system failures using fault tree analysis (2016)
3. Kaiser, B., Gramlich, C., Förster, M.: State/event fault trees—a safety analysis model for software-controlled systems. Reliab. Eng. Syst. Saf. **92**, 1521–1537 (2007)
4. Seifert, D.: Model-based Refactoring for Component Fault Trees (2020) Accessed 27 Dec. 27
5. Velasco Moncada, D.S.: Hazard-driven realization views for component fault trees. Softw. Syst. Model. **19**, 1465–1481 (2020)
6. Sabaliauskaite, G., Mathur, A.P.: Aligning Cyber-Physical System Safety and Security. In: Cardin, MA., Krob, D., Lui, P., Tan, Y., Wood, K. (eds) Complex Systems Design & Management Asia. Springer, Cham (2015). https://doi.org/10.1007/978-3-319-12544-2_4
7. Fovino, I.N., Masera, M., De Cian, A.: Integrating cyber attacks within fault trees. Reliab. Eng. Syst. Saf. **94**, 1394–1402 (2009)
8. Steiner, M., Liggesmeyer, P.: Combination of safety and security analysis-finding security problems that threaten the safety of a system (2013)
9. Kumaraswamy, N., Ekin, T., Park, C., Markey, M.K., Barner, J.C., Rascati, K.: Using a Bayesian Belief Network to detect healthcare fraud. Expert Syst. Appl. **238**, 122241 (2024)
10. Pirbhulal, S., Gkioulos, V., Katsikas, S.: Towards integration of security and safety measures for critical infrastructures based on bayesian networks and graph theory: a systematic literature review. Signals **2**, 771–802 (2021)
11. Alzu'bi, A., Alomar, A., Alkhaza'leh, S., Abuarqoub, A., Hammoudeh, M.: A review of privacy and security of edge computing in smart healthcare systems: issues, challenges, and research directions. Tsinghua Sci. Technol. **29**, 1152–1180 (2024)
12. Ness, S., Khinvasara, T.: Emerging threats in cyberspace: implications for national security policy and healthcare sector. J. Eng. Res. Rep. **26**, 107–117 (2024)
13. Niv, Y., Tal, Y.: Risk Management and patient safety processes in a healthcare organization. In: Patient Safety and Risk Management in Medicine: From Theory to Practice, pp. 129–174. Springer (2024)
14. Anghel, I., et al.: Smart environments and social robots for age-friendly integrated care services. Inter. J. eNviron. Res. Public Health **17**, 3801 (2020)

15. Rivera, R., Amorim, M., Reis, J.: Robotic services in smart cities: an exploratory literature review. In: 2020 15th Iberian Conference on Information Systems and Technologies (CISTI), pp. 1–7. IEEE (2020)
16. Gültekin-Várkonyi, G., Kertész, A., Váradi, S.: Application of the general data protection regulation for social robots in smart cities. Handbook of Smart Cities, pp. 1–25 (2020)
17. SecuRoPS. https://ife.no/en/project/securops-2/
18. Oruma, S.O., Sánchez-Gordón, M., Colomo-Palacios, R., Gkioulos, V., Hansen, J.K.: A systematic review on social robots in public spaces: threat landscape and attack surface. Computers. **11**, 181 (2022)
19. Ayele, Y.Z., Chockalingam, S., Lau, N.: Threat actors and methods of attack to social robots in public spaces. In: Moallem, A. (eds) HCI for Cybersecurity, Privacy and Trust. HCII 2023. LNCS, vol. 14045. Springer, Cham (2023). https://doi.org/10.1007/978-3-031-35822-7_18
20. Oruma, S.O., Ayele, Y.Z., Sechi, F., Rødsethol, H.: Security aspects of social robots in public spaces: a systematic mapping study. Sensors. **23**, 8056 (2023)
21. Sabaliauskaite, G., Mathur, A.P.: Aligning Cyber-Physical System Safety and Security. In: Cardin, MA., Krob, D., Lui, P., Tan, Y., Wood, K. (eds.) Complex Systems Design & Management Asia. Springer, Cham (2015). https://doi.org/10.1007/978-3-319-12544-2_4
22. Fovino, I.N., Masera, M., De Cian, A.: Integrating cyber attacks within fault trees. Reliab. Eng. Syst. Saf. **94**(9), 1394–1402 (2009)
23. Steiner, M., & Liggesmeyer, P. (2013). Combination of safety and security analysis-finding security problems that threaten the safety of a system
24. Chockalingam, S., Pieters, W., Teixeira, A., Khakzad, N., van Gelder, P.: Combining Bayesian Networks and Fishbone Diagrams to Distinguish Between Intentional Attacks and Accidental Technical Failures. In: Cybenko, G., Pym, D., Fila, B. (eds.) Graphical Models for Security. GraMSec 2018. LNCS, vol. 11086. Springer, Cham (2019). https://doi.org/10.1007/978-3-030-15465-3_3
25. Shanmugam, B., Azam, S.: Risk assessment of heterogeneous IoMT devices: a review. Technologies **11**(1), 31 (2023)
26. Pritika, S., B., & Azam, S.: Risk evaluation and attack detection in heterogeneous IoMT devices using hybrid fuzzy logic analytical approach. Sensors **24**(10), 3223 (2024)
27. Gebrie, M.T., Abie, H.: Risk-based adaptive authentication for IoT in smart home. In: Proceedings of the 11th European Conference on Software Architecture: Companion Proceedings, pp 102–108 (2017) (ISBN 978-1-4503-5217-8).
28. Sodhro, A.H., Lakhan, A., Pirbhulal, S., Groenli, T.M., Abie, H.: A Lightweight Security Scheme for Failure Detection in Microservices IoT-Edge Networks. In: Suryadevara, N.K., George, B., Jayasundera, K.P., Roy, J.K., Mukhopadhyay, S.C. (eds.) Sensing Technology. LNEE, vol. 886. Springer, Cham (2022).https://doi.org/10.1007/978-3-030-98886-9_31
29. MIT Technology Review. A patient has died after ransomware hackers hit a German hospital (2020). https://www.technologyreview.com/2020/09/18/1008582/a-patient-has-died-after-ransomware-hackers-hit-a-german-hospital/
30. Oakley, A.: HIPAA, HIPPA, or HIPPO: what really is the heath insurance portability and accountability act? Biotechnol. Law Rep. **42**(6), 306–318 (2023)
31. Mohammad Amini, M., Jesus, M., Fanaei Sheikholeslami, D., Alves, P., Hassanzadeh Benam, A., Hariri, F.: Artificial intelligence ethics and challenges in healthcare applications: a comprehensive review in the context of the European GDPR mandate. Mach. Learn. Knowl. Extract. **5**(3), 1023–1035 (2023)
32. González-Villa, J., et al.: Decision-support system for safety and security assessment and management in smart cities. Multimedia Tools Appli. **83**(22), 61971–61994 (2024)
33. Li, Z., Jin, D., Hannon, C., Shahidehpour, M., Wang, J.: Assessing and mitigating cybersecurity risks of traffic light systems in smart cities. IET Cyber-Phys. Syst. Theory Appli. **1**(1), 60–69 (2016)

34. Prabhu, S., Kumar, A.: Security and privacy risk with social robotics. In: Information Technology Security and Risk Management, pp. 146–152. CRC Press (2024)
35. Denning, T., Matuszek, C., Koscher, K., Smith, J.R., Kohno, T.: A spotlight on security and privacy risks with future household robots: attacks and lessons. In: Proceedings of the 11th International Conference on Ubiquitous Computing, pp. 105–114 (September 2009)
36. Ayele, Y.Z., Chockalingam, S., Lau, N.: Threat actors and methods of attack to social robots in public spaces. In: Moallem, A. (eds.) HCI for Cybersecurity, Privacy and Trust. HCII 2023. Lecture Notes in Computer Science, vol. 14045. Springer, Cham (2023). https://doi.org/10.1007/978-3-031-35822-7_18
37. Oruma, S.O., Ayele, Y.Z., Sechi, F., Rødsethol, H.: Security aspects of social robots in public spaces: a systematic mapping study. Sensors **23**(19), 8056 (2023)
38. Cooper, S., Di Fava, A., Vivas, C., Marchionni, L., Ferro, F.: ARI: the social assistive robot and companion. In: 2020 29th IEEE International conference on robot and human interactive communication (RO-MAN), pp. 745–751. IEEE (August 2020)
39. Ragno, L., Borboni, A., Vannetti, F., Amici, C., Cusano, N.: Application of social robots in healthcare: review on characteristics, requirements, technical solutions. Sensors **23**(15), 6820 (2023)
40. González-González, C.S., Violant-Holz, V., Gil-Iranzo, R.M.: Social robots in hospitals: a systematic review. Appl. Sci. **11**(13), 5976 (2021)
41. Chockalingam, S., Hadžiosmanović, D., Pieters, W., Teixeira, A., van Gelder, P.: Integrated Safety and Security Risk Assessment Methods: A Survey of Key Characteristics and Applications. In: Havarneanu, G., Setola, R., Nassopoulos, H., Wolthusen, S. (eds.) Critical Information Infrastructures Security. CRITIS 2016. LNCS, vol. 10242. Springer, Cham (2017). https://doi.org/10.1007/978-3-319-71368-7_5
42. Yang, T. H., Qin, J., Li, Z.X.: Public safety risk assessment of power investment project based on fuzzy set and DS evidence theory. In: E3S Web of Conferences, vol. 143, p. 02009. EDP Sciences (2020)
43. Chen, C., Reniers, G., Khakzad, N.: Integrating safety and security resources to protect chemical industrial parks from man-made domino effects: a dynamic graph approach. Reliab. Eng. Syst. Saf. **191**, 106470 (2019)
44. Cavalheiro, A.C., et al.: Specification of supervisory control systems for ventricular assist devices. Artif. Organs **35**(5), 465–470 (2011)
45. Kayan, H., Nunes, M., Rana, O., Burnap, P., Perera, C.: Cybersecurity of industrial cyber-physical systems: a review. ACM Comput. Surv. (CSUR) **54**(11s), 1–35 (2022)
46. Hemsley, K. E., Fisher, E.: History of industrial control system cyber incidents (No. INL/CON-18-44411-Rev002). Idaho National Lab.(INL), Idaho Falls, ID (United States) (2018)
47. Abdelkader, S., et al.: Securing modern power systems: implementing comprehensive strategies to enhance resilience and reliability against cyber-attacks. Results Eng., 102647 (2024)
48. Song, G., Khan, F., Yang, M.: Integrated risk management of hazardous processing facilities. Process. Saf. Prog. **38**(1), 42–51 (2019)
49. Boikanyo, K., Zungeru, A.M., Sigweni, B., Yahya, A., Lebekwe, C.: Remote patient monitoring systems: Applications, architecture, and challenges. Scientific African **20**, e01638 (2023)
50. European Commission. Critical infrastructure resilience at EU-level (2024). https://home-affairs.ec.europa.eu/policies/internal-security/counter-terrorism-and-radicalisation/protection/critical-infrastructure-resilience-eu-level_en
51. Kriaa, S., Bouissou, M., Colin, F., Halgand, Y., Pietre-Cambacedes, L.: Safety and Security Interactions Modeling Using the BDMP Formalism: Case Study of a Pipeline. In: Bondavalli, A., Di Giandomenico, F. (eds.) Computer Safety, Reliability, and Security. SAFECOMP 2014. LNCS, vol. 8666. Springer, Cham (2014). https://doi.org/10.1007/978-3-319-10506-2_22

Cybersecurity Adaptive and Continuous Authentication in Healthcare

5G Beyond for Healthcare: Leveraging AI/ML and Diverse Datasets for Cybersecurity

Ali Hassan Sodhro[1](✉), Muhammad Irfan Younas Mughal[2], and Muhammad Javed Iqbal[3]

[1] Department of Computer Science, Kristianstad University,
29188 Kristianstad, Sweden
ali.hassansodhro@hkr.se
[2] Computer System Engineering, Sukkur IBA University, Sukkur 65200, Pakistan
irfan.younas@iba-suk.edu.pk
[3] Institute of Space Science and Technology, University of Karachi,
Karachi 75270, Pakistan
javiqbal@uok.edu.pk

Abstract. The rapid adoption of 5G networks, space networks, and Internet of Things (IoT) technologies in healthcare has significantly expanded the attack surface for cybersecurity threats. This evolving landscape demands robust defense mechanisms that can anticipate and neutralize sophisticated cyber-attacks. Artificial Intelligence (AI), Machine Learning (ML), and Deep Learning (DL) technologies are pivotal in developing such advanced cybersecurity solutions. A critical factor influencing the effectiveness of these AI/ML models is the quality and diversity of the datasets used in their training. This paper presents a systematic review of various datasets used for AI/ML-based cybersecurity model training across multiple domains, with a focus on 5G networks, IoT healthcare, and space networks. By employing a structured Goal-Question-Metric (GQM) methodology and Quasi-Gold Standard (QGS) validation, we assessed the characteristics, applications, and limitations of real, synthetic, and hybrid datasets in enhancing cybersecurity measures. The review identifies key trends, gaps, and future research directions, highlighting the need for more diverse datasets, standardized benchmarks, and privacy-preserving techniques. Our findings offer insights into improving the resilience of AI/ML models for cybersecurity, guiding the development of more effective and adaptable defense strategies across emerging network technologies.

Keywords: Cybersecurity · AI · ML · DL · Models · Datasets · 5G Networks · IoT Healthcare

1 Introduction

The widespread adoption of 5G, space networks, and Internet of Things (IoT) technologies in healthcare has substantially expanded the attack surface, creating new vulnerabilities that can be exploited by cybersecurity threats. This increased exposure demands robust and innovative defense mechanisms. In this evolving landscape, AI, Machine Learning (ML), and Deep Learning (DL) technologies are crucial for developing advanced cybersecurity solutions capable of anticipating and neutralizing threats [1].

A critical determinant of the effectiveness of these AI/ML models is the quality and diversity of the datasets used in their training. Datasets play a foundational role in shaping the ability of models to recognize patterns, adapt to new threats, and generalize across different scenarios. This paper reviews the application of various datasets across these technologies, assessing their impact on model performance and adaptability to specific cybersecurity challenges [2]. However, existing literature on AI/ML cybersecurity models often lacks a comprehensive analysis of the datasets used for training these models, particularly across multiple domains. This gap limits the understanding of the dataset characteristics that are essential for developing effective cybersecurity solutions tailored to diverse environments.

Therefore, this review aims to systematically evaluate the types of datasets (real, synthetic, hybrid, and other) employed in AI/ML model training for cybersecurity across various contexts, including 5G networks, space networks, and IoT healthcare. To address this gap, a systematic review process was employed, utilizing the Quasi-Gold Standard (QGS) approach to ensure that the literature search captured the most relevant and impactful studies. The QGS method involves using a set of key studies as benchmarks to validate the search strategy, thus improving the accuracy and completeness of the review process.

In Fig. 1, we present a hierarchical structure of cybersecurity model training, illustrating the foundational role of datasets in AI/ML-based cybersecurity applications. This figure is an original contribution, conceptualized to emphasize how the quality and characteristics of datasets influence the subsequent layers of model development and practical application across domains like 5G, IoT, and healthcare. The hierarchical structure is designed to show the progression from foundational datasets to more complex, domain-specific integrations, such as 5G and IoT healthcare.

While the figure is a novel representation, it is informed by existing principles in AI/ML model training and cybersecurity practices. Previous works have highlighted the importance of data quality and model adaptability in cybersecurity [3], which influenced the development of this hierarchical framework. This conceptual model aims to visually connect these principles, providing a new perspective on how datasets drive effective cybersecurity model training across various domains.

This paper is organized into several sections, each designed to provide a clear and detailed insight into our review process and findings. Following this introduction, Sect. 2 outlines the review protocol and methodology used. Section 3 and 4 reviews our fifty relevant studies that detail the type of datasets used and their particular applications in 5G networks, space networks, and IoT health care. Concluding sections then try to discuss the implications of such findings,

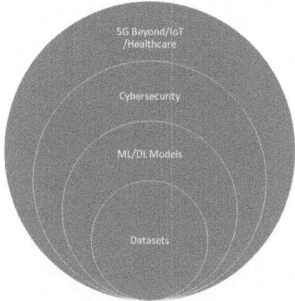

Fig. 1. The training of the cybersecurity model here is in a hierarchical representation, from foundational datasets that are well and truly centered to broader application areas such as 5G, IoT, and healthcare.

identify the final research gaps, and propose some future research directions to further develop the effectiveness of AI/ML models for cybersecurity.

2 Review Protocol

We back our review with the GQM approach [4]. The GQM approach of the manuscript is mainly adopted during the Planning Phase, basing the groundwork for the review. In general, GQM involves specifying the goal of a review, elaborating questions which must be answered in order to determine if the goal has been met, and finally defining metrics to measure whether the goal has been met. The GQM approach, in this context, has been used to structure the research effort in the Planning Phase of our manuscript to systematically review the literature on AI/ML cybersecurity across domains like 5G, space networks, and IoT healthcare. Questions identified, such as what types of datasets used and their characteristics, guide the review process. Metrics are subsequently leveraged to evaluate if the review is good at addressing these questions.

2.1 Planning Phase

We searched in databases like IEEE Xplore, ACM Digital Library, and PubMed [5], to look for publications from 2022 since our aim was related to recent development. The Goal-Question-Metric (GQM) approach was used to structure the review process systematically in this phase. The aim is to conduct an exhaustive search on works dealing with AI/ML models used in different perspectives around these networks and the third network, i.e., health IoT. In order to tighten the search and selection process, specific questions were geared towards finding what types of datasets are utilized or if they describe attributes about them–also focused on their application in cybersecurity. To address this, metrics were set up to gauge relevance and quality given that publications had already commenced on the subject from 2022 onwards, in order for it to be recent advances today, and an attempt was made to provide studies detailing dataset usage.

Database Selection: We chose three main databases for a full literature review: IEEE Xplore, ACM Digital Library, and PubMed [6]. These databases were chosen for their relevance and coverage in the fields of cybersecurity, artificial intelligence (AI), machine learning (ML), deep learning (DL), and healthcare research.

- IEEE Xplore is widely recognized as a leading repository for engineering, computer science, and technology-related research, offering access to high-quality, peer-reviewed papers, especially in the areas of AI/ML applications and 5G network technologies.
- ACM Digital Library provides a comprehensive collection of computing and information technology literature, making it an ideal source for studies on cybersecurity and network technologies.
- PubMed is a well-established database for biomedical and healthcare research, ensuring coverage of studies that involve IoT healthcare and medical cybersecurity. The selection of these databases aimed to ensure a balanced inclusion of studies covering technical, computational, and healthcare aspects of the research topic. The use of these well-known and respected databases helps to guarantee that the review encompasses relevant and high-quality studies.

Inclusion and Exclusion Criteria: To ensure the quality and relevance of the studies included in this review, we established the following inclusion and exclusion criteria. The criteria were guided by the GQM approach, ensuring that the studies selected were aligned with the established goals, answered the research questions, and met the quality metrics.

Studies published from 2022 onwards were included to ensure the review reflects the latest advancements in the field. Only studies that explicitly addressed the use of AI, ML, or DL models for cybersecurity across the domains of 5G networks, space networks, or IoT healthcare were considered. The selected studies needed to provide details about the datasets used, including their type (real, synthetic, or hybrid) and application in training AI/ML models for cybersecurity. Only studies published in English were included to maintain consistency in language across the review.

Studies that did not provide sufficient information on the datasets utilized for AI/ML model training were excluded. Research that focused on unrelated topics, such as general AI applications not involving cybersecurity or studies centered solely on non-digital healthcare solutions, was excluded. Duplicate studies found across multiple databases were removed to ensure that each included study was unique. Studies that were not published in peer-reviewed journals, conference proceedings, or reputable sources were excluded to ensure the quality of the included literature.

The above criteria guided the systematic selection and screening of studies to ensure that the review included relevant, high-quality research addressing the use of datasets in AI/ML-based cybersecurity across 5G networks, space networks, and IoT healthcare.

2.2 Execution Phase

We chose three main databases for a full literature review: IEEE Xplore, ACM Digital Library, and PubMed.

((("cybersecurity" OR "security" OR "privacy" OR "differential privacy") AND ("AI" OR "ML" OR "DL" OR "artificial intelligence" OR "machine learning" OR "deep learning" OR "neural networks") AND ("dataset*" OR "training data" OR "feature extraction") AND ("5G network*" OR "space network*" OR "IoT healthcare" OR "Internet of Things"))

An elaborate process for this search string has been tested on a pool of pioneering QGS studies [7], to confirm it will retrieve the most relevant literature for AI/ML cybersecurity training with different network technologies. The Quasi-Gold Standard (QGS) approach is a technique that evaluates the performance of search strategies for systematic literature reviews. This includes generating a list of core QGS studies that are determined necessary and must be captured by the search string run. The role of QGS is to guarantee the searching strategy's sensitivity (ability to identify all relevant records) and specificity (ability to correctly exclude irrelevant studies).

Identifying specific important studies based on the topic is used in QGS, which we applied for categorizing cybersecurity training methods of AI/ML models applicable to 5G networks, space networks, and IoT healthcare domains in our manuscript. This served as a baseline against which the search string could be validated. To verify the search strategy was successful, we tested the search string to query whether all QGS studies were able to be retrieved. Repeating the QGS process led to the refinement of the search string for optimal sensitivity by adding or changing keywords after comparing how well our initial search measured against screened studies. Quality control using both methods reduced screening time and decreased false negatives. Thus, the QGS method is important in that it adds to the quality and completeness of the literature search, making the review more systematic and reliable. The inclusion of QGS in the manuscript ensures that the search process is robust, reduces the chances of missing key studies, and supports the validity of the findings by using a well-tested search strategy (Fig. 2).

Building upon the refined search string's ability to retrieve highly relevant literature, the figure illustrates a systematic review protocol for cybersecurity datasets, segmented into three phases: Planning, Execution, and Evaluation & Reporting, and outlines the progression from initial search to final study selection. In the Planning Phase, a structured approach was established using the Goal-Question-Metric (GQM) method to guide the review framework, with a clearly defined search strategy and keywords to ensure comprehensive coverage. The Execution Phase involved conducting searches across IEEE Xplore, ACM Digital Library, and PubMed using the refined search string and a Quasi-gold Standard (QGS) technique to enhance sensitivity and specificity, thus ensuring the retrieval of relevant studies from multiple disciplines. The low number of

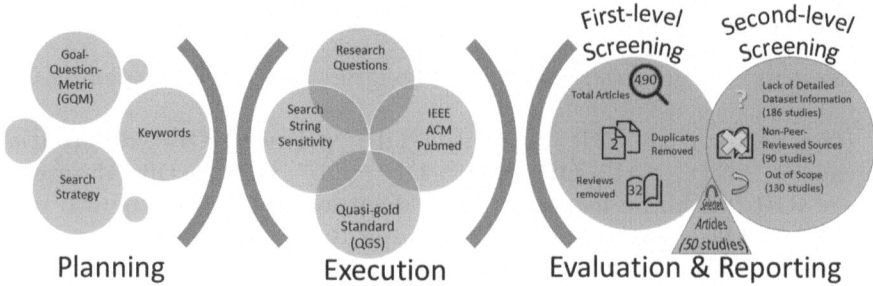

Fig. 2. Review protocol for cybersecurity datasets, segmented into Planning, Execution, and Evaluation & Reporting phases, illustrating the systematic study selection process including first-level and second-level screenings, with details on the number of studies reviewed and excluded at each stage.

duplicates removed (2) confirms the appropriateness of the selected databases, capturing a diverse set of relevant studies without significant overlap.

In the Evaluation & Reporting Phase, the screening process was carried out in two levels: the first-level screening excluded **2 duplicates and 32 review papers, with the low number of reviews further supporting the motivation for conducting this review, as it indicates a scarcity of comprehensive reviews in this field. Additionally, the high number of studies lacking dataset details (186) highlighted a significant gap in the literature, emphasizing the need for more research providing comprehensive dataset descriptions for AI/ML cybersecurity. The second-level screening excluded 90 non-peer-reviewed studies and 130 out-of-scope studies, indicating the necessity for focused studies that specifically address AI/ML applications in cybersecurity across 5G, space networks, and IoT healthcare. Ultimately, 50 studies met all the inclusion criteria, validating the effectiveness of the systematic approach and revealing important gaps in the existing literature.

2.3 Evaluation and Reporting Phase

After the initial search, duplicates and studies not meeting the inclusion criteria were removed. We distilled the results down to fifty essential articles for in-depth analysis [8]. Our inquiry is structured around four research questions(RQ).

RQ1: What types of datasets are available for 5G network cybersecurity model training?
RQ2: What types of datasets ares utilized in space networks to combat cybersecurity challenges?
RQ3: Which datasets are employed specifically in the IoT healthcare domain?
RQ4: What essential characteristics must datasets possess for effective cybersecurity model training? The inclusion of QGS studies in refining our search string ensures the robustness and applicability of our review process, thoroughly addressing the strategic deployment of datasets in cybersecurity model training.

Following the QGS approach, we wanted to fine-tune and validate our search strategy by manually screening a set of pivotal studies sourced from significant venues [9]. This involves complementing the automatic search results by manually identifying key studies from well-regarded publication sources. The purpose is to ensure that crucial and influential studies are included in the review, especially those that may not have been captured by the automatic search due to limitations in search engine algorithms or indexing. By manually selecting pivotal studies from recognized venues, the review ensured that it did not miss out on significant research related to AI/ML cybersecurity applications in areas such as 5G, space networks, and IoT healthcare. Not only has this approach improved The quality of the books selected is only partial. Gold standard (QGS) analyzes were used to further confirm the analysis thread. This helped us optimize the search string for increased sensitivity and specificity with changes such as wording changes and some additions Specific keywords such as 'IoT datasets' To focus on relevant areas, such as 'IoT security datasets'. Evidence of the effectiveness of this increased search string Analysis using QGS was achieved by sensitivity and scoring 100% on both precision metrics, indicating that the sequential surveys were successfully retrieved All relevant assessments identified in the QGS. This methodical technique guarantees that our search strategy is thorough and accurate for the review, and that it finds the most pertinent literature sources.

3 Review Findings and Analysis

Following a strict application of our review protocol, we have identified and critically analyzed fifty studies that address the use of datasets in training AI/ML models for cybersecurity in various domains, including but not limited to 5G networks, space networks, and IoT healthcare. To clarify, the fifty studies were used as the basis for the analysis presented in this section, while the references section includes the studies directly cited to support the specific findings and discussions. This differentiation helps distinguish between the broader set of studies analyzed for insights and the key studies explicitly referenced in the manuscript. These studies utilized different types of datasets: real, synthetic, and hybrid. The primary objective of these studies is to enhance the effectiveness and reliability of AI models in detecting and mitigating cyber threats in these advanced technological environments. Fourteen articles focus on using real datasets, which emphasize practical relevance and improve the generalizability of AI models. These datasets are typically collected from actual network traffic, real-time IoT data, and other live environments. Ten articles espouse the Use of synthetic data sets, specifically developed to simulate certain IoT and network conditions. These are scalable datasets and customized for the training of models. Within controlled environments. Two peer-reviewed journal articles explore hybrid datasets, which combine real and synthetic data to use the benefits of both. By adding the real-world Hybrid datasets lend a sensible base to models, hence ensuring and thereby generalize soundly to real situations. Hence, this authenticity gives rise to Capturing the variability and complexity in real-world network traffic or healthcare contexts data, which is crucial for identifying complex cyber threats. Conversely, In contrast, synthetic elements facilitate the production of controlled situations facilitate the modeling of various assault scenarios or infrequent occurrences that may not be available in the real-world datasets. For instance, hybrid datasets in IoT healthcare can Use both clinical data appropriately anonymized and generated data designed to mimic different types of attacks, including data poisoning or malicious attacks [10]. Attempts of access. This serves to train the AI models such that within a comprehensive framework which encompasses regular as well as special situations, reinforces robustness to a wide range of attacks. In 5G networks also, Hybrid datasets may contain real network traffic along with artificially induced attack vectors. For example, DDoS attacks or signal jamming. Those help in testing the models' ability to Identify and respond to various types of network anomalies.

Hybrid datasets are especially useful for domains such as space networks, in which actual data is frequently hard or unavailability to obtain. By integrating Real satellite communication data plus simulation data created for potential scenarios. Cyber threats, for example jamming and spoofing, hybrid datasets help create robust AI Models designed to overcome the unique difficulties that space network operations pose. Thus, hybrid datasets offer a balanced training environment that leverages the strengths of both real and synthetic data to develop high-performing and adaptable AI/ML models for cybersecurity.

These datasets aim to ensure robust and high-performing models by providing a comprehensive training environment. Twenty four articles utilize various other datasets that do not fall strictly into real, synthetic, or hybrid categories. In Fig. 3, the "other" category of dataset types encompasses datasets that do not fit strictly into the real, synthetic, or hybrid classifications but still play a role in training AI/ML models for cybersecurity. These may include datasets that are derived from anonymized or obfuscated data sources, such as network traffic data with altered IP addresses to ensure privacy, or augmented datasets, where data augmentation techniques (e.g., noise addition, scaling) are used to expand the training set artificially [11]. Other dataset types may also refer to transformed or pre-processed datasets where specific features have been extracted or modified to focus on certain characteristics (e.g., frequency patterns in signal data for radio frequency fingerprinting). While these datasets may not fully replicate real-world scenarios or controlled synthetic environments, they still contribute to model training by enhancing data diversity and helping to generalize the model's performance across different conditions. The inclusion of "other" datasets highlights the diversity of data sources used in AI/ML cybersecurity research and reflects efforts to balance data privacy concerns with the need for effective model training.

These include novel and advanced dataset techniques for cybersecurity applications as shown in below Fig. 3. To further structure the findings of this review, we categorize the identified studies into different research questions (RQs) that guide the exploration of specific dataset types and their applications across cybersecurity domains. Each research question delves into critical aspects such as dataset availability for specific network technologies (5G and space), essential characteristics of datasets for effective AI model training, and specific datasets used in IoT healthcare cybersecurity. In the following sections, we explicitly address each research question by referencing the relevant findings from the reviewed studies, emphasizing the practical relevance and challenges associated with real, synthetic, and hybrid datasets in different domains

RQ1: What types of datasets are available for 5G network cybersecurity model training?
This section answers RQ1 by discussing the datasets used for 5G network cybersecurity, such as the 5G-NIDD dataset. As detailed in Sect. 3.1, this dataset captures real network traffic and various types of network attacks, such as SYN Flood, UDP Flood, and ICMP Flood, making it invaluable for training AI/ML models to detect and mitigate cyber threats in 5G environments.

RQ2: What types of datasets are utilized in space networks to combat cybersecurity challenges?
To address RQ2, Sect. 3.1 also explores space network datasets like the Satellite-Terrestrial Integrated Network (STIN) dataset. This dataset reflects the operational challenges specific to satellite communications, such as long transmission delays and high error rates, providing a controlled environment for training AI models to detect space network-specific threats, including jamming and spoofing attacks.

RQ3: Which datasets are employed specifically in the IoT healthcare domain?
RQ3 is answered in Sect. 3.2, where the paper discusses various datasets used in IoT healthcare. Examples include real IoT healthcare data that enhances privacy in federated learning models, as explored in Javeed et al., and simulated healthcare data for intrusion detection systems, discussed in Sáez-de-Cámara et al. These datasets demonstrate how AI/ML models can be trained to address the cybersecurity challenges unique to IoT healthcare, ensuring data privacy and system security.

RQ4: What essential characteristics must datasets possess for effective cybersecurity model training?
RQ4 is explored throughout Sects. 3.2 and 3.3, where we examine key characteristics of real, synthetic, and hybrid datasets. For instance, real datasets provide practical relevance and robustness, synthetic datasets offer scalability and control over training environments, and hybrid datasets combine the strengths of both to provide comprehensive training. Studies like those by Sánchez et al. and Javeed et al. highlight the need for diverse and high-quality datasets that address real-world security challenges while maintaining model accuracy and efficiency.

3.1 Answering RQ1 and RQ2: Datasets for 5G and Space Networks

To answer the research questions regarding the types of datasets available for 5G and space networks for training AI/ML models in cybersecurity, we conducted

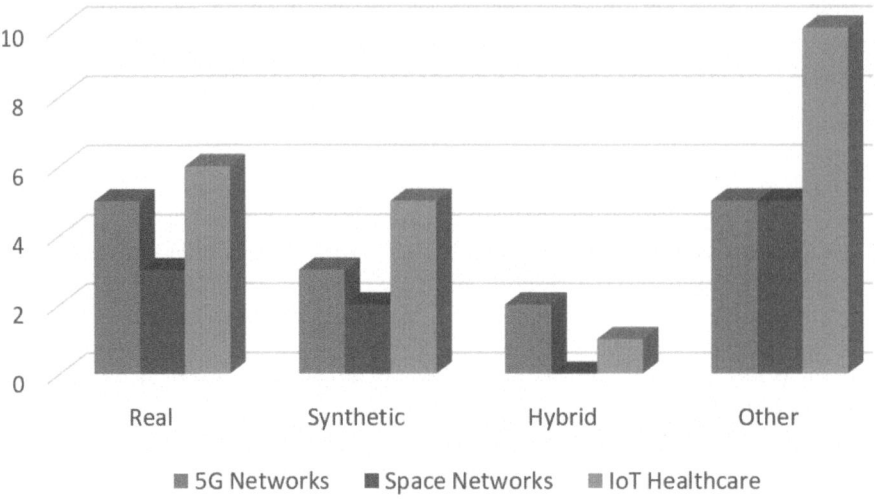

Fig. 3. Distribution of real, synthetic, hybrid and other datasets used for AI/ML models in cybersecurity across 5G Networks, Space Networks, and IoT Healthcare.

an extensive review of relevant studies. For training AI/ML models in cybersecurity specifically tailored to 5G networks, datasets like the 5G Network Intrusion Detection Dataset (5G-NIDD) are commonly used [12]. This dataset is generated from actual network traffic in 5G environments and includes various types of network attacks such as SYN Flood, UDP Flood, and ICMP Flood. Data is collected to provide a lifelike simulation of benign and malicious traffic patterns within the network. In this way, it is possible to develop and test AI/ML models that might help in the effective detection and containment of cyber threats targeting 5G networks. This detailed logging of the datasets involved the traffic types, attack vectors, and timestamps indispensable to model the learning to detect and respond to anomalies on the network [12–14]. In Industrial IoT (IIoT) frameworks based on 5G, [15] took advantage of the MNIST and Fashion-MNIST datasets for the improvement in model training. This approach dealt with federated learning (FL) through differentially private (DP) mechanisms and used sparse responses to achieve accuracy while keeping the data private. These examples are illustrative of the fact that federated learning has actually proven itself in practice, outperforming other methods known to date as set for IIoT systems on real-world data. A study [16] of edge-based malware detection in IIoT Systems Mobile edge computing (MEC) integrated with 5G has facilitated the opportunity to perform efficient data processing and real-time malware detection in mobile devices. Although the study did not specify any particular dataset type, it focused on how 5G and edge computing can improve cybersecurity in IIoT settings. Research [17] explored the area of security improvements in IIoT systems, RF fingerprinting was employed. End-to-end framework enhanced 5G enabled the solution by addressing issues related to interference and noise, thus leading communications a robust and secure way. Although the specific types of data sets were not described, it was about employing RFID-scalable techniques with an advanced 5G RF context for securing the IIoT systems. Moreover, in the study, a reinforcement learning approach to integrating honeypots into ultra-dense beyond 5G networks was introduced. This study implemented honeypots to place in 5G networks for detecting and preventing various attacks by using encryption keys on the edge of IoT data enabled with Machine Learning (ML) [18], investigated other types of research utilized simulated traffic datasets that serve as training/validation datasets processed into the security model. For space networks, the datasets used are designed to reflect the unique operational challenges of satellite communications, which include long transmission delays, high error rates, and specific security threats not typically seen in terrestrial networks. One notable dataset is the Satellite-Terrestrial Integrated Network (STIN) dataset, which simulates satellite network environments for cybersecurity training. This dataset includes features tailored to the hybrid nature of satellite-terrestrial networks, such as varying signal strengths and the unique protocols used in satellite communications. The STIN dataset is utilized to train models on recognizing and responding to threats that are specifically engineered to exploit the vulnerabilities of satellite networks, such as spoofing and jamming attacks. This preparation helps ensure the robustness of cybersecurity measures in the face of the unique conditions encountered in space network operations [19].

3.2 Answering RQ3: Datasets for IoT Healthcare

Securing one of the most sensitive forms of data, it is vital that IoT healthcare also applies AI/ML models in its cybersecurity practices. In our review, we systematized the different types of datasets in this area and concentrated on how they impact cybersecurity. In the meantime [20] proposed to further private data by adopting federated learning with differential privacy against gradient leakage in cross-silo environments. By utilizing the real-world IoT healthcare data to train models, this approach proved practical for use in specific and delicate environments like real-life hospital scenarios. This demonstrated better privacy maintenance and invariance to the data leakage problem, showcasing applications of real datasets toward model reliability and security under IoT healthcare ecosystems. These datasets provide a practical context for training the models, enabling them to learn from real-world data patterns, which enhances the model's ability to detect and respond to potential cyber threats more effectively. By training on real datasets, which reflect the complexities and variability of actual network traffic or IoT data, the models become better equipped to identify anomalies, suspicious behaviors, or attack patterns that may not be present in synthetic datasets alone. This improves the model's robustness and reduces its vulnerability to sophisticated threats by preparing it to handle real-life scenarios, rather than reducing the threats themselves. In this context, the focus is on minimizing the model's susceptibility to undetected threats, ensuring a higher degree of vigilance and resilience in real-time applications. Hence, a related study also proposed an innovative federated learning algorithm to improve model training efficiency in IoT healthcare [21]. Using the better particle swarm optimization approach on medical IoT datasets provided an increase of approximately 10% in model accuracy and a decrease up to eight times in training time while keeping patient data privacy. This study argues that using specialized datasets like medical IoT data is useful for achieving higher accuracy and efficiency in federated learning models.

This research [22] focuses on enhancing intrusion detection systems (IDS) in IoT healthcare scenarios. Experimentation using the IDS models to check their ability to detect cyber threats from simulated healthcare data has been performed, providing more control over the system. The authors of this paper highlighted the benefits of having the ability to develop, pilot, and validate, through the use of simulated datasets, security algorithms prior to their actual use in an operational setting under controlled conditions [23]. Another study results have shown high accuracy for the proposed machine learning models in classifying applications based on real health care network traffic data, thus largely improving security and reliability of IoT e-health systems [24]. This work indicates that the use of real network traffic data to train advanced machine learning models is imperative to achieve effective security within IoT-based health care systems. [25] is a research that introduced an intrusion detection framework using federated learning on IoT healthcare with real datasets and synthetic ones to model the participants. Keeping privacy concerns in mind, mixed datasets were able to strike a balance between privacy and robustness of models, thereby achieving better intrusion detection without compromising data confidentiality. This provided insight into combining real and synthetic datasets to create a complete and fair training landscape for creating cyber defense models. All these studies have collectively shown variance in real, synthetic, and hybrid datasets of real application and the effectiveness in improving cybersecurity within IoT-based healthcare systems. Real datasets are practically relevant and authentic; synthetic datasets entail controlled testing environments; and hybrid datasets draw the strength from both to ensure robust high-performing AI models. This is directed to answer directly the posed research question: **Which datasets are employed specifically in the IoT healthcare domain?** Thus, the finding suggests that a combination of real, synthetic, and hybrid datasets be collected and developed to train effective AI/ML models for securing IoT healthcare systems.

3.3 Answering RQ4: Characteristics of Effective Cybersecurity Datasets

In our comprehensive review, we focus on the characteristics of the data used in training AI/ML models in cybersecurity within the domain of IoT healthcare. This analysis is related to the derived answer to our research question: "What are the identified cybersecurity datasets used specifically in IoT healthcare applications?" The works focused on the importance of various types of data sets, real, synthetic, and hybrid data sets and their effectiveness in maximizing security measures. The first work is by Sánchez et al. [20], which proposed a learning method to defend against leakage of the gradient through learning while maintaining data privacy. The practical relevance and performance in real-world scenarios are demonstrated using real-world IoT healthcare data for model training. The results show that privacy preservation is significantly improved and robustness against data leakage enhanced, which would be great progress in IoT healthcare security research. In another related study, Sáez-de-Cámara et al. [26] leverage Federated Learning to enhance the efficiency of model training in IoT healthcare. They show remarkable enhancements in model accuracy and time to train models on medical IoT data and maintain privacy of data as well through the use of an enhanced technique of particle swarm optimization. The technique developed provides a compromise between efficiency and privacy, integrated with the level of data in the dataset and its heterogeneous nature. Javeed et al. [22] target enhancing intrusion detection systems (IDS) over IoT-based healthcare environments. Training the IDS models by applying simulated healthcare data will allow for controlled experiments and validation of the proposed algorithm effectiveness to detect various cyber threats. The datasets are scalable, and it can be tested under various hypothetical scenarios. Cunha et al. [24] dealt with the challenge of encrypted network traffic in IoT healthcare systems. The Machine Learning models achieve a high level of accuracy in application labeling through real healthcare network traffic data, and this increases the general security and dependability of such a system, whereby practical relevance of real dataset use avails realistic training data. Finally, it used federated learning as a method for privacy-preserving intrusion detection in software-defined networks, using mixed real and synthetic datasets to balance privacy concerns and model robustness. This approach ensures that effective intrusion detection is achieved while maintaining data confidentiality, which means that hybrid datasets are of utmost importance in cybersecurity and provide a robust training environment for AI models.

3.4 Key Trends in Cybersecurity Dataset Utilization

The datasets described in Table 1 have been classified in four categories: real, synthetic, general, and hybrid. For instance, MNIST and Fashion-MNIST are real datasets derived directly from real data points. They form an indispensable part of modeling for responses coming out of the conditions that really exist in the world. Synthetic datasets, on the other hand, are artificially constructed to simulate certain scenarios or conditions, which can create a relevant environment to test and enhance models in cybersecurity under hypothetical threats. The diversity in the dataset types highlights the general spectrum that is represented in cybersecurity challenges, from general threats to network security to very specific subjects like malware detection and RF interference.

Table 1. Summary of Datasets Used in Cybersecurity Model Training

Dataset	Dataset Type	Cybersecurity Use	Domain	ML/DL Model Used	Ref.
MNIST and Fashion-MNIST	Real	General Cybersecurity	5G	Federated Learning (FL)	[27]
IoT healthcare data	Real	Data Privacy	IoT Healthcare	Federated Learning (FL)	[16]
Medical IoT data	Real	Data Privacy	IoT Healthcare	Federated Learning (FL)	[28]
Simulated healthcare data	Synthetic	Intrusion Detection	IoT Healthcare	Intrusion Detection Systems (IDS)	[23]
Healthcare network traffic data	Real	Network Traffic Analysis	IoT Healthcare	Application Labeling via ML	[24]
Mixed real and synthetic datasets	Hybrid	Intrusion Detection	IoT Healthcare	Intrusion Detection via FL	[22]
5G-NIDD	Real	Malware Detection	5G	LSTM Autoencoders	[12]
KDD dataset	Real	Intrusion Detection	IoT Healthcare	SVM	[14]
STIN and UNSW-NB15	Hybrid	Intrusion Detection	Satellite Networks	RF-SFS-GRU	[19]

While Table 1 presents ten representative studies, the remaining studies were still integral to the overall review and analysis. These studies contributed to identifying broader trends and insights but were not individually included in the table to maintain a focused presentation. The studies in Table 1 were chosen specifically to illustrate key findings and examples across diverse domains, dataset types, and applications, while the analysis of all fifty studies informed the conclusions and guided the interpretation of results. The remaining studies provided additional context and helped to validate the observed patterns, ensuring a robust and comprehensive understanding of the literature. These datasets cover domains on emerging network technologies such as 5G and the Industrial Internet of Things, including critical sectors like IoT healthcare. The above domains illustrate the practicality and applicability of the datasets, as they are solely developed to fulfill the requirements needed in each technology. The table also showcases various AI/ML models that have been applied to make the most out of these datasets: Federated Learning, SVMs, and LSTM Autoencoders, for a capacity of optimizing security measures according to the dataset. In addition, it dovetails with the research questions set out in the table (RQ1 to RQ4) as structured insight on how each dataset deals with specific aspects of cybersecurity. The alignment with this area will support the pinpointing of contributions from each dataset in the improvement of model training and response capabilities under different cybersecurity threats. Besides that, it also allows reference listing for each entry in the dataset to allow the readers to check the original study where these datasets were being discussed before and can be further explored.

4 Discussion

The findings of this review shed light on insightful revelations into the current state of dataset usage for training models related to AI, ML, and DL in the domain of cybersecurity across various technological sectors such as 5G networks, space networks, and IoT healthcare. The findings of this review provide critical insights into the role of datasets in training AI, ML, and DL models for cybersecurity across various technological domains. This section distinctly covers How the results speak to each of the four research questions in the study.

Addressing RQ1: Datasets about 5G networks indicate that results confirm RQ1 was addressed by identifying key datasets for 5G network security, such as the 5GNIDD It's a collection of real-time network traffic data for cybersecurity. The dataset provides detailed measurements of various forms of network attacks-for instance SYN Flood, UDP Flood, as well as non-malicious traffic patterns, enable AI/ML models to In fully active 5G settings, gain skill to detect and respond to cybersecurity threats. The utilization of authentic datasets such as 5G-NIDD underscores the practical significance and Only actual data can improve the strength and reliability of. Security models for the 5G landscape.

Addressing RQ2: Data Sources for Space Networks To answer RQ2, the study emphasizes the STIN (Satellite-Terrestrial Integrated Network) dataset as a This is an important factor for securing space networks. The results indicate that unique challenges space networks face, such as high transmission delays and error rates, which require specialized datasets. The STIN dataset combines real and synthetic data to simulate satellite network conditions, thus giving a robust scenario for training models of AI in the defense against jammers and impersonation. Such datasets are essential for the advancement of cybersecurity solutions. Customized to address the unique operational difficulties inherent in space networks.

Addressing RQ3: Characteristics of Effective Cybersecurity Datasets For RQ3, the results describe the characteristics of datasets necessary for Effectiveness of cybersecurity model training: It criticizes three elementary datasets categories: authentic, artificial, and mixed. Authentic datasets, such as real-time network traffic, provide the practical relevance and feasible usability of artificial intelligence models. Artificial Synthetical Data sets offer the scalability to scale the number of different attack vectors and network conditions, which happens to be highly useful in controlled environments. Hybrid datasets merge the strengths of each other, ensuring thorough Training models to scenarios where authentic data may be lacking or Sensitive. These findings highlight the need for diverse and high-quality datasets that offer scalability, relevance, and adaptability for cybersecurity applications.

Addressing RQ4: Datasets for IoT Healthcare The findings related to RQ4 show that IoT healthcare relies on a variety of datasets-real, synthetic, and hybrid-to secure its systems against cyber threats. For example, real healthcare network traffic data is used in intrusion detection systems (IDS) to identify potential threats, while simulated healthcare data allows for controlled testing and validation of security algorithms before deployment in real-world environments. Hybrid datasets strike a balance between privacy concerns and security robustness, which is particularly important in healthcare, where patient data confidentiality is critical. These datasets ensure that AI/ML models are effectively trained to handle the cybersecurity challenges unique to IoT healthcare.

4.1 Interpretation of Results

Our results indicate that most of these environments use real datasets that reflect actual network conditions and cyber threats: IoT and 5G. These datasets provide a practical context in training the models, which increases the model's ability to be vigilant to real-time threats and decrease any potential threat. On the contrary, space networks mostly ask for hybrid datasets due to their peculiar challenges in operations, including lengthy transmission delays and error rates that are so high that real-world data combined with synthetic scenarios would be required to create a robust cybersecurity solution.

This is why synthetic datasets, especially in controlled conditions like IoT healthcare, are being adopted at a scale for simulations that real datasets alone would be incapable of. This becomes essential to test cybersecurity measures against varied attack vectors and network conditions in view of increasing the reliability of cybersecurity models before their actual implementation in real-world scenarios.

4.2 Implications of Findings

It is in this respect that the effectiveness of models trained on real datasets for IoT and 5G applications comes out, which then further underscores the importance of data authenticity in the practice of cybersecurity. Real datasets enable the models to handle actual data and scenarios they are likely to encounter, thus improving their practical utility and reliability.

Secondly, the use of synthetic and hybrid datasets highlights the innovative approaches in training models where real data might be limited or too sensitive to use, such as in space networks and certain IoT healthcare applications. These datasets help in creating controlled environments that can rigorously test the resilience of cybersecurity models against sophisticated cyber-attacks, which is critical for the advancement of security measures in these high-stakes fields.

Thirdly, the study's findings advocate for the continuous development and sharing of high-quality, diverse datasets within the cybersecurity community. This could lead to more effective AI/ML solutions, as diverse datasets help in training more robust models capable of generalizing well across different scenarios and attacks. The idea that training ML/DL models on a variety of datasets-including real, synthetic, and hybrid data-can lead to more effective cybersecurity solutions is based on the rationale that diverse datasets provide a broader range of scenarios for the model to learn from. Real datasets capture the complexity and variability of actual cyber threats, while synthetic datasets allow for controlled testing with diverse and rare attack types that may not be present in real data. Hybrid datasets, combining the strengths of both, can therefore offer a comprehensive training environment. Studies have shown that models trained on heterogeneous datasets often perform better when it comes to generalizing across different conditions and identifying anomalies in varied data sources [29–31], While the current literature supports this trend, further research is needed to quantify the impact of dataset diversity on specific performance metrics in cybersecurity applications. This presents an opportunity for future studies to systematically evaluate how different types of datasets contribute to the effectiveness of ML/DL models in detecting and mitigating cyber threats.

However, while the potential benefits of dataset diversity are supported by some existing studies, this concept requires further empirical validation. Future research should explore how different combinations of real, synthetic, and hybrid datasets impact specific performance metrics, such as accuracy, generalizability, and resilience against various cyber threats. Addressing this gap through experimental studies could provide a more solid foundation for best practices in using diverse datasets to enhance model performance.

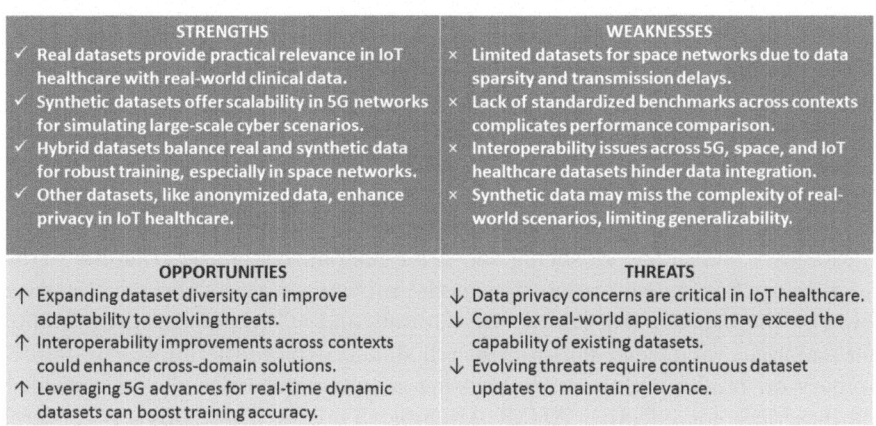

Fig. 4. SWOT chart summarizing the strengths, weaknesses, opportunities, and threats associated with different dataset types (real, synthetic, hybrid, other) used in cybersecurity across 5G networks, space networks, and IoT healthcare, with context-specific examples.

4.3 Limitations of Current Research

The SWOT analysis in Fig. 4 summarizes the strengths, weaknesses, opportunities, and threats associated with the use of different dataset types (real, synthetic, hybrid, other) in cybersecurity applications across 5G networks, space networks, and IoT healthcare. The figure highlights context-specific examples to show how each dataset type performs in different domains, such as the practical relevance of real datasets in IoT healthcare, the scalability benefits of synthetic datasets in 5G networks, and the balanced approach of hybrid datasets in addressing the unique challenges of space networks. This detailed analysis aims to provide a clearer understanding of the potential advantages and limitations of each dataset type while identifying areas where improvements and future research could enhance the effectiveness of AI/ML-based cybersecurity solutions. This analysis highlights:

Strengths: Datasets derived from actual network traffic significantly enhance model accuracy and have practical relevance. Synthetic datasets provide scalability for diverse scenarios, and hybrid datasets combine these benefits, supporting robust cybersecurity training. Weaknesses: The limited scope of datasets fails to cover the full spectrum of cybersecurity threats, and the lack of standardized benchmarks hinders model evaluation and comparison. Limited interoperability between datasets also restricts comprehensive, cross-domain analysis. Opportunities: Increasing dataset diversity can help reflect the evolving cyber threat landscape more accurately, enhancing the adaptability of ML/DL models. Combining real, synthetic, and hybrid datasets prepares models to detect a wider range of threats across various conditions. 5G advancements further improve dataset functionality and model training by enabling the collection of large volumes of real-time data from diverse sources, resulting in richer datasets.

For example, 5G networks facilitate massive IoT deployments where connected devices generate continuous data streams, creating dynamic datasets that better mirror real-world conditions. This data can be used for training AI models to detect threats based on real-time network traffic and device behaviors. Additionally, 5G's low-latency capabilities support edge computing, allowing for the rapid generation and use of labeled datasets to keep models up-to-date.

Moreover, 5G's network slicing allows for customized datasets tailored to different network segments, enhancing model robustness across diverse scenarios. However, the benefits of using diverse datasets and 5G technologies require further empirical validation. Future research should explore the impact of dataset diversity on model performance, focusing on comparative studies to establish best practices for effective AI/ML training. Threats: Data privacy concerns persist, especially with datasets containing sensitive information. The dynamic nature of cyber threats necessitates continual updates to datasets and training methods. The study presents a comprehensive review of datasets for training AI/ML models in cybersecurity across 5G networks, space networks, and IoT healthcare, but several limitations pose potential threats to validity [32]. Internal validity could be affected by selection bias, as the systematic search strategy focused on studies from 2022 onward and specific keywords, potentially excluding relevant older studies or those using different terminology. To mitigate this, the Quasi-Gold Standard (QGS) approach was used to validate the search string, although unintentional exclusions may still exist. External validity is limited since the findings may not generalize to areas outside the reviewed domains, such as traditional enterprise networks, despite including various dataset types (real, synthetic, hybrid) to offer a broader perspective. Construct validity is challenged by inconsistencies in dataset descriptions across studies, where some provided detailed characteristics while others briefly mentioned the dataset type, potentially impacting the analysis. Standardized criteria were applied to assess datasets consistently, yet variability in reporting remains a concern. Conclusion validity may be affected by reliance on representative examples discussed in Sect. 3, which focused on key trends from the broader set of studies. While these examples were chosen to illustrate themes such as dataset diversity and application domains, the overall analysis was based on all fifty studies to derive trends and insights, with measures taken to ensure a balanced evaluation despite potential limitations.

5 Conclusion

This review has thoroughly analyzed the use of datasets in training AI, ML, and DL models across cybersecurity contexts like 5G, space networks, and IoT healthcare. Our findings categorize dataset types-real, synthetic, and hybrid-each crucial for their respective domains. The conclusions presented in this review are grounded in the analysis of all fifty studies, which helped to validate and contextualize the key findings. Real datasets are essential in IoT and 5G for addressing real-world threats, while synthetic and hybrid datasets provide scalability and controlled environments, vital for space networks and specialized IoT healthcare applications. Below, we summarize how each of the research questions (RQs) was addressed: RQ1 asked, "What types of datasets are available for 5G network cybersecurity model training?" This review identified several key datasets, such as the 5G-NIDD dataset, which provides real-time network traffic data for 5G environments. These datasets include logs of cyberattacks, such as SYN Flood and UDP Flood, which are used to train AI/ML models to detect and respond to real-world cybersecurity threats in 5G networks. The use of such real datasets ensures that models are robust and capable of addressing practical cybersecurity challenges in 5G networks.

RQ2 inquired, "What types of datasets are utilized in space networks to combat cybersecurity challenges?" The review identified the STIN (Satellite-Terrestrial Integrated Network) dataset, which combines real and synthetic data to simulate space network conditions. This dataset addresses the unique challenges of space networks, such as long transmission delays and high error rates, and is used to train models to detect specific threats like jamming and spoofing attacks. The inclusion of both real and synthetic data in these datasets ensures that Cyber-security solutions are so specifically tailored for the specifics of space networks.

RQ3 focused on "Which datasets are employed specifically in the IoT healthcare domain?" The review revealed that IoT healthcare systems rely on a mix of real, synthetic, and hybrid datasets. Real traffic data of a healthcare network This is crucial for improving the accuracy of intrusion detection systems (IDS), whereas simulated healthcare data provides a controlled environment for testing cybersecurity. Models before field deployment. Hybrid datasets strike a balance between privacy and security robustness, making them highly effective in training AI models to secure IoT healthcare systems while maintaining patient confidentiality.

RQ4 sought to find out "What essential characteristics must datasets possess for effective cybersecurity model training?" Datasets must be diverse, flexible, and relevant to application situations. Real Datasets demonstrate practical significance by accurately representing actual traffic and attack scenarios. Patterns and synthetic datasets support scalability while controlling the testing environment. Hybrid datasets integrate the advantage of each type, ensuring a thorough analysis model training. These are characteristics of great value to ensure that AI/ML models prove to be effective across the domains of various cyber threats.

The study stresses how the construction of datasets must be continually updated. To keep up with the changing cyber threat landscape, striking a balance between data accessibility and privacy, especially in sensitive areas like healthcare. However, The review also underlines several important challenges such as dataset biases and less geographic and operational diversification. These are the problems must be addressed in order to cultivate resilient and equitable AI models.

This research should, however lead to standardization in datasets, enhance real-time data processing and, integrating new technologies aimed at improving cyber security. This enhances these dimensions for the cyber security industry. To combat sophisticated threats, making AI-powered security solutions both The review is proactive, by nature, resilient, and an appeal for enhanced inclusivity and rigorous research to ensure a safe internet.

Acknowledgment. This work is supported by Kristianstad University, Sweden, Sukkur IBA University, Pakistan and COST Action CA22168-Physical layer security for trustworthy and resilient 6G systems (6G-PHYSEC), and COST Action CA22104-Behavioral Next Generation in Wireless Networks for Cyber Security (BEiNG-WISE).

References

1. Apruzzese, G., et al.: The role of machine learning in cybersecurity. Digital Threats, **4**(1) (2023). Article 8
2. Jada, I., Mayayise, T.O.: The impact of artificial intelligence on organisational cyber security: an outcome of a systematic literature review. Data Inf. Manag. 100063 (2023)
3. Meng, X.: Advanced AI and ml techniques in cybersecurity: Supervised and unsupervised learning, reinforcement learning, and neural networks in threat detection and response. Appl. Comput. Eng. **82**, 1–5 (2024)
4. Basili, V., Caldiera, G., Rombach, H.: The Goal Question Metric Approach. Wiley 1994)
5. Gusenbauer, M.: Search where you will find most: Comparing the disciplinary coverage of 56 bibliographic databases. Scientometrics **127**, 2683–2745 (2022)
6. Gusenbauer, M., Haddaway, N.R.: Which academic search systems are suitable for systematic reviews or meta-analyses? Evaluating retrieval qualities of google scholar, pubmed, and 26 other resources. Res. Synthes. Meth. **11**(2), 181–217 (2020)
7. Zhang, H., Babar, M.A., Tell, P.: Identifying relevant studies in software engineering. Inf. Software Technol. **53**(6), 625–637 (2011)
8. Kitchenham, B., Charters, S.: Guidelines for performing systematic literature reviews in software engineering. Technical report, EBSE Technical Report (2007)
9. Jalali, S., Wohlin, C.: Systematic literature studies: database searches vs. backward snowballing. In: Proceedings of the ACM-IEEE International Symposium on Empirical Software Engineering and Measurement, pp. 29–38 (2012)
10. Khan, M.M., Alkhathami, M.: Anomaly detection in IoT-based healthcare: machine learning for enhanced security. Sci. Rep. **14**(1), 5872 (2024)

11. Zion, Y., Aharon, P., Dubin, R., Dvir, A., Hajaj, C.: Enhancing encrypted internet traffic classification through advanced data augmentation techniques. arXiv preprint arXiv:2407.16539 (2024)
12. Samarakoon, S., et al.: 5G-NIDD: a comprehensive network intrusion detection dataset generated over 5g wireless network (2022)
13. Agrafiotis, G., Makri, E., Lalas, A., Votis, K., Tzovaras, D., Tsampieris, N.: A deep learning-based malware traffic classifier for 5g networks employing protocol-agnostic and PCAP-to-embeddings techniques. In: *Proceedings of the 2023 European Interdisciplinary Cybersecurity Conference*, EICC '23, pp. 193–194, New York, NY, USA. Association for Computing Machinery (2023)
14. Tamilarasi, M., Karthick, R., Sanjeev, R., Sasidharan, S.: Intrusion detection in healthcare domain using machine learning. Int. J. Health Sci. **6**(S4), 5861–5872 (2022)
15. Cui, L., et al.: Boosting accuracy of differentially private federated learning in industrial IoT with sparse responses. IEEE Trans. Industr. Inf. **19**(1), 910–920 (2023)
16. Deng, X., et al.: Edge-based IIoT malware detection for mobile devices with offloading. IEEE Trans. Industr. Inf. **19**(7), 8093–8103 (2023)
17. Gul, O.M., et al.: Secure industrial IoT systems via RF fingerprinting under impaired channels with interference and noise. IEEE Access **11**, 26289–26307 (2023)
18. Author, M., et al.: Strategic honeypot deployment in ultra-dense beyond 5g networks: a reinforcement learning approach
19. Azar, A.T., Shehab, E., Mattar, A.M., et al.: Deep learning based hybrid intrusion detection systems to protect satellite networks. J. Network Syst. Manag. **31**(82) (2023)
20. Sánchez, P.M.S., et al.: A fine-grained differentially private federated learning against leakage from gradients. IEEE Trans. Dependable Secure Comput. **21**(2), 573–584 (2024)
21. Sáez de Cámara, X., et al.: Boosted federated learning based on improved particle swarm optimization. IEEE Trans. Dependable Secure Comput. **21**(1), 186–203 (2024)
22. Javeed, D., et al.: Enhancing intrusion detection systems for IoT and cloud environments using a growth optimizer algorithm and conventional neural networks. ACM Trans. Internet Technol. (2023)
23. Javeed, D., et al.: A softwarized intrusion detection system for IoT-enabled smart healthcare system. ACM Transactions on Internet Technology (2023)
24. Cunha, A.A., et al.: Extensible machine learning for encrypted network traffic application labeling via uncertainty quantification. In: Proceedings of the 18th ACM International Symposium on QoS and Security for Wireless and Mobile Networks (Q2SWinet '22), pp. 63–70 (2022)
25. Raza, M., et al.: Federated learning for privacy-preserving intrusion detection in software-defined networks. IEEE Access **12**, 69551–69567 (2024)
26. Cámara, X.S., Flores, J.L., Arellano, C., Urbieta, A., Zurutuza, U.: Gotham testbed: a reproducible IoT testbed for security experiments and dataset generation. IEEE Trans. Dependable Secure Comput. **21**(1), 186–203 (2023)
27. Yamany, W., Moustafa, N., Turnbull, B.: OQFL: an optimized quantum-based federated learning framework for defending against adversarial attacks in intelligent transportation systems. IEEE Trans. Intell. Transp. Syst. **24**(1), 893–903 (2021)

28. Houssein, E.H., Sayed, A.: Boosted federated learning based on improved particle swarm optimization for healthcare IoT devices. Comput. Biol. Med. **163**, 107195 (2023)
29. Cui, Z., Godwin, N., Chao, K.-M., Chung, J.-Y., Tsai, C.-F.: A functional data service framework for integrating heterogeneous data sources. In: 2008 32nd Annual IEEE International Computer Software and Applications Conference, pp. 1150–1155 (2008)
30. Zhang, Q., Jian, D., Xu, R., Dai, W., Liu, Y.: Integrating heterogeneous data sources for traffic flow prediction through extreme learning machine. In: 2017 IEEE International Conference on Big Data (Big Data), pp. 4189–4194 (2017)
31. Xu, W., Chen, J., Zhang, X.J., Xiong, L., Chen, H.: A framework of integrating heterogeneous data sources for monthly streamflow prediction using a state-of-the-art deep learning model. J. Hydrol. **614**, 128599 (2022)
32. Yu, C., Ohlund, B.: Threats to validity of research design (2010)

A Secure Privacy-Preserving Multimodal Continuous Authentication Protocol for Healthcare Systems

Ahmed Fraz Baig[1,3]($^{\boxtimes}$), Sigurd Eskeland[2], Bian Yang[3], and Patrick Bours[3]

[1] Biofy AS, Gjøvik, Norway
ahmed.baig@biofy.no
[2] University of Agder, Grimstad, Norway
[3] Norwegian University of Science and Technology (NTNU), Gjøvik, Norway

Abstract. eHealth systems require usable but more robust authentication mechanisms to balance security and usability. Continuous authentication is a security mechanism that passively conducts user authentication throughout the session. Continuous authentication may best fit healthcare systems as it enhances security and improves usability by seamlessly authenticating users. It may face limitations when only one modality is supported, such as keystroke dynamics, gait dynamics, touch dynamics, etc. These modalities collect and utilize user-sensitive data containing information about user behavioral and contextual activities, and other user-sensitive attributes, e.g., user gender, age, etc., may also be derived from such data, which causes privacy concerns. Continuous authentication using multiple modalities may overcome the limitations of a single modality at the cost of compromising user privacy. The more modalities we employ, the more privacy we compromise.

In this paper, we propose a privacy-preserving protocol that supports continuous authentication using multiple modalities. Our proposed protocol protects 1) user-sensitive attributes and 2) the privacy of the type of modality (such as user activities). The biometric performance of the proposed protocol is determined in the following ways: a) individually, on two public datasets, a keystroke dynamics dataset, and a swipe gesture dataset, and b) multimodal, by combining swipe gesture and keystroke data. For multimodal, instead of computing cosine similarity for each action, we comput ed the extended similarity based on multiple (k) keystroke and swipe gesture actions. The experimental evaluation proves that our proposed protocol with the extended technique performs better than the original cosine similarity. The proposed protocol offers efficient biometric performance, low communication and computation costs, and security in the presence of a semi-honest authentication server, malicious users, and external adversaries.

Keywords: Privacy · Cryptographic protocol · Continuous authentication · Homomorphic encryption · eHealth systems

1 Introduction

Traditional healthcare systems are being transformed into eHealth systems, which enable access to healthcare services remotely and improve the quality of care. Technological enhancements also open various security incidents in different domains. Security breaches are happening more consistently and frequently. Healthcare systems face various security and privacy challenges; patient personal data, such as patient records, histories, information about medication, etc., are stored in these systems, and they are sensitive and require robust security mechanisms.

There are different reasons for such security threats, such as utilizing a poor authentication method is considered as one of the leading causes of security vulnerabilities. Traditional authentication mechanisms utilize PINs/passwords, tokens, or biometrics, and authentication takes place once at the beginning of a session. These authentication mechanisms sometimes fail to deal with certain security vulnerabilities, such as when credentials get stolen, successful brute-force attacks, a device remains unattended for a while, and an illegitimate user uses it, etc. Continuous authentication enhances security by passively monitoring users' contextual and behavioral activities throughout the session. This ensures that only the legitimate user is allowed to use the device, and it locks the device whenever suspicious activities are detected. Contextual modalities authenticate a user by continuously monitoring physical and logical locations, network data, operating systems, cookies, etc. The behavioral biometrics utilize data about user behavioral actions such as keystrokes, swipe gestures, gait dynamics, stylometry, etc. [1].

Individual modalities of continuous authentication, e.g., keystroke, swipe gesture, gait dynamics, GPS data, etc., may face limitations when a user does not perform modality-specific action, and restricting the user to perform an explicit action reduces usability. For instance, only contextual modalities cannot detect an imposter when no contextual change happens, such as when a device remains unlocked in an office or home and an imposter uses it. Similarly, a single modality of behavioral biometrics may face limitations when the imposter user does not perform modality-specific action; for example, continuous authentication only relies on gait dynamics, but the imposter does not perform that action.

Security can be strengthened by achieving continuous authentication using multiple modalities (multimodal), such as multiple behavioral biometrics or behavioral biometrics in combination with contextual modalities [1]. Using multiple modalities together may strengthen security but also open various privacy challenges. Outsourcing such data to a third party causes privacy concerns. The first privacy challenge is that these data contain information about a user's physical and logical locations, cookies, and other device data. Other sensitive information, such as user age, gender, handedness, etc., can be inferred from such data. Second, revealing the type of the modality itself is a privacy concern, even if the features are protected. For instance, the type of modality reveals the user's daily life actions and activities, such as typing information of keystrokes, swipe gestures, gait dynamics, location information, etc. Based on such activities, user profiling can be done maliciously, and this makes continuous authentication privacy-invasive. Such sensitive data require privacy-preserving storage and processing (GDPR Art. 9 [2]).

Existing schemes for privacy-preserving continuous authentication have high communication overhead, which proves their impracticality to many applications. One reason for their impracticality is that the existing schemes do not differentiate between continuous and static authentication. They attempt to solve privacy problems by proposing cryptographic schemes similar to static authentication. Note that, for continuous authentication, the authentication decision cannot be made on a single action, but in static authentication, the decision is made after a single action. Instead of using normal cosine similarity, we use the idea of extended similarity and make the authentication decision after multiple (k) actions (activities). This solution is very suitable for continuous authentication and requires low communication between the user and the authentication server.

Motivation

Healthcare systems deal with patients and medical professionals. These systems require secure and usable authentication because patients may likely have certain injuries or forget the credentials (usernames, PINs, passwords, etc.) due to some diseases, including mild cognitive impairment (MCI), mental stress, or any other similar age-specific disease. Such diseases may cause the refusal of service due to the failure in authentication, resulting in a bad user experience.

Considering usability and privacy issues, this paper proposes a usable and privacy-preserving continuous authentication protocol that authenticates users passively and does not require their attention during authentication. The proposed protocol uses the Paillier cryptosystem with (2,2) threshold decryption to protect the privacy of 1) user activities and 2) user-sensitive attributes. The proposed protocol protects the privacy of reference templates from both parties; due to the (2,2) threshold, the decryption of a ciphertext is only possible when both parties collaborate.

This paper assumes strong security assumptions, including a malicious user who may deviate from the protocol, external adversaries who may considered active or passive adversaries and may modify or replay the transmitted messages, and a semi-honest authentication server. This article makes the following contributions:

1. The protocol can be utilized for continuous authentication using (any) single and multiple modalities without any modifications.
2. Low communication and computation overhead, efficient biometric performance, and provides the same accuracy as is in the plaintext domain.
3. Security in the presence of the malicious user, semi-honest authentication server, and external adversaries.

The rest of the paper is organized as follows; we discuss the related work in Sect. 2; preliminaries are discussed in Sect. 3; Sect. 4 presents generic authentication scheme; the privacy-preserving protocol is proposed in Sect. 5; performance evaluation is presented in Sect. 6, Sect. 7 concludes the paper and discusses future work.

2 Related Work

This section discusses the literature survey of privacy-preserving continuous authentication protocols. Safa et al. [3] proposed a generic privacy-preserving scheme for implicit authentication using contextual data. Their proposed protocol protects privacy using additive homomorphic encryption with order-preserving symmetric encryption (OPSE). They use Average Absolute Deviation to determine the dissimilarity between authentication and enrollment features. Domingo-Ferrer et al. [4] proposed a protocol that computes a private set intersection between a set of enrollment features and the authentication features. Their setting is based on additive homomorphic encryption property, and the proposed protocol does not require a private key. Eskeland [5] showed that the Domingo-Ferrer et al. protocol cannot withstand two attacks: by the first attack, the authentication server can obtain the enrollment feature vector, and by the second attack, the probe data can be revealed. Shahandashti et al. [6] presented a privacy-preserving protocol that utilizes contextual data for implicit authentication. Their settings are based on two cryptosystems; 1) additive homomorphic encryption, which protects the privacy of contextual data, and 2) order-preserving symmetric encryption which enables keeping the plaintext values in ciphertext in a manner that preserves their relative order.

Govindarajan et al. [7] used additive homomorphic encryption to propose a privacy-preserving authentication scheme for behavioral features. They determined the dissimilarity between the probe and enrollment features using Scaled Euclidean Distance (SED) and Scaled Manhattan Distance (SED). Their proposed schemes are based on Damgård et al. [8] cryptosystem and Erkin et al. [9] protocol. The Erkin et al. [9] protocol utilizes Damgård et al. [10,11] protocol for the privacy-preserving comparison. Sitová et al. [12] presented a database for behavioral authentication; they also proposed an authentication scheme that uses a fuzzy commitment scheme [13] to protect the behavioral data. Balagani et al. [14] extended a similar idea presented by Govindarajan et al. to propose a privacy-preserving protocol for keystroke dynamics. They presented privacy-preserving matching algorithms known as Absolute ("A") and Relative ("R") measures; their settings are also based on Damgård et al. [10,11] protocol. Wei et al. [15] proposed an implicit authentication scheme to protect the privacy of behavioral features. They used Paillier cryptosystem and computed a cosine similarity in the encrypted domain, where the authentication server determines the outcome by decrypting the final similarity scores. Eskeland and Baig [16] proved that the Wei et al. protocol fails to provide privacy against honest-but-curious authentication server and also vulnerable to active attack. Baig et al. [17] proposed two authentication protocols utilizing homomorphic encryption with an oblivious transfer protocol (OT). Their first protocol uses homomorphic encryption, and the second protocol uses homomorphic encryption with an OT. The homomorphic operations are performed on the device; the user and the authentication server collaborate to get the final result.

Table 1. Notation

U	User	AS	Authentication server
$\vec{a_i}$	Reference vector of ith activity	$\vec{p_i}$	Probe vector of ith activity
d_s	Server private key share	d_u	Client private key share
$\overrightarrow{[a_i]}$	Encrypted enrollment vector	x, y	Random numbers generated by AS
γ_i	Random number generated by U	$[x]$	Encryption of plaintext x
N	Total number of activities	m	total elements in one vector

3 Preliminaries

This section discusses the security goals and adversarial model.

3.1 Security Goals

The privacy-preserving continuous authentication protocol achieves the following goals:

1. The authentication server must not learn stored enrollment and probe vectors.
2. The user must not learn the enrollment vectors.
3. During the authentication, the authentication server must not learn the information about the modality used for authentication.
4. The protocol should resist external adversarial attacks.

3.2 Adversarial Model

We consider the following types of adversaries:

- *Semi-honest authentication server.* We assume that the authentication server is semi-honest, and attempts to learn user biometric and contextual features and user activities.
- *Malicious user.* We assume that the user may be malicious and can deviate from the protocol. A malicious user may try to learn enrollment feature vectors.
- *External adversary.* We assume that the external adversary has control over the public channel and can replay the transmitted messages.

3.3 Building Blocks

To propose a privacy-preserving protocol, we consider the following building blocks:

Cosine similarity measures the similarity between sequences of elements in the vectors. It computes the inner dot product of a sequence of elements in vectors, and the dot product is divided by the product of the lengths of vectors. Assume $\vec{a_i}=(a_{ij},...,a_{im})$ and $\vec{p_i}=(p_{ij},...,p_{im})$ are two vectors, the cosine similarity between $(\vec{a_i}, \vec{p_i})$ is defined as

$$\cos(\vec{a_i}, \vec{p_i}) = \frac{\sum_{i=1}^{m} a_{ij}p_{ij}}{\sqrt{\sum_{j=1}^{m} a_{ij}^2}\sqrt{\sum_{j=1}^{m} p_{ij}^2}} \qquad (1)$$

A cosine similarity of 1 indicates that $\vec{a_i}$ and $\vec{p_i}$ are exactly similar, where 0 indicates complete dissimilarity between two vectors.

4 Multimodal Continuous Authentication Using Extended Similarity

The continuous authentication scenario consists of two phases: 1) an enrollment phase and 2) an authentication phase. Each modality may have a different range of values in the feature vector; the features are scaled in the same range; we refer the reader to the following references [18,19] for the details about feature scaling techniques.

During the enrollment phase, reference feature vector $\vec{a_i} = (a_{i1},...,a_{im})$ for each activity is constructed and in accordance with the cosine similarity their normalized value $A_i = \sqrt{\sum_{j=1}^{m} a_{ij}^2}$ is computed for each activity i; for instance, a swipe-gesture or a single keystroke pattern is considered one activity.

We propose a continuous authentication scheme based on multiple modalities, so instead of a single reference template, we construct N templates $(\vec{a_i}, A_i)_{i=1}^{N}$ and assign an index i to each, where N is the total number of activities (templates) and $1 \leq i \leq N$. Each reference template consists of a vector $(\vec{a_i})$ of m elements and their normalized value A_i of each activity, where j is the jth element of ith activity and $1 \leq j \leq m$. The number of elements in the vector depends on the particular activity, such as a vector of swipe gesture contains less elements than a vector of a keystroke pattern.

During the authentication phase, probe vector $\vec{p_i} = (p_{i1},...,p_{im})$ is sampled and corresponding $P_i = \sqrt{\sum_{j=1}^{m} p_{ij}^2}$ is computed for the performed activity. A similarity between $\vec{a_i}$ and $\vec{p_i}$ is computed. One cannot make the authentication decision based on the outcome of a single activity, such as a single swipe gesture, a single keystroke, etc. Instead of using a single activity, a decision can be made based on k activities, where $2 \leq k \leq N$. The extended similarity is computed as follows [17]:

$$S = \frac{S'}{S''} = \frac{\sum_{i=1}^{k}\sum_{j=1}^{m} a_{ij}p_{ij}}{\sum_{i=1}^{k} A_i P_i} = \frac{\sum_{i=1}^{k}\sum_{j=1}^{m} a_{ij}p_{ij}}{\sum_{i=1}^{k}\sqrt{\sum_{j=1}^{m} a_{ij}^2}\sqrt{\sum_{j=1}^{m} p_{ij}^2}} \quad (2)$$

The sum of dot products for k activities in the numerator is computed as $S' = \sum_{i=1}^{k}\sum_{j=1}^{m} a_{ij}p_{ij}$ and the sum of products of their corresponding normalized values in the denumerator is computed as $S'' = \sum_{i=1}^{k} A_i P_i$. The similarity scores are determined by performing a division as $S = S'/S''$, S is compared to a threshold (T), if $(S > T)$ is true, then the user is accepted.

There are different ways to compute cosine similarity; for instance, [15,20] normalized features first and then computed the cosine similarity as a dot product. In this paper, we compute extended cosine similarity, where the numerator and denumerator are computed separately for k activities as shown in the Eq. 2; this offers the following advantages:

a) *Low communication cost.* This allows computing the similarity of k activities, the privacy-preserving protocol based on this approach offers very low communication cost, as it enables transmission after k activities instead of after each activity, as stated in the later Sect. 5.3.
b) *Better biometric performance.* It results in a very good performance regarding Equal Error Rate (EER) compared to computing cosine similarity based on a single activity.
c) *Better security.* As biometric features have a low entropy, we can blind features in the numerator and denumerator in a way so that they do not affect the result; see Sect. 5.3.

5 Proposed Protocol

This section proposes a privacy-preserving authentication protocol that protects the privacy of feature vectors and user activities. The proposed protocol consists of a setup phase, an enrollment phase, and an authentication phase. The proposed protocol is shown in Fig. 1.

5.1 Setup Phase

The Paillier Cryptosystem with (2,2)-Threshold Decryption. A trusted third party creates and securely distributes public and private keys, where the private key λ is blinded with randomly chosen $\beta \in \mathbb{Z}_n^*$ and $\theta = \lambda\beta \bmod n$. θ is added to the public key (g, n), where $g = n + 1$, $n = pq$. The product $\lambda\beta$ is split into two shares d_u and d_s, where the user holds d_u, and the authentication server holds d_s, so that $\lambda\beta = d_u + d_s$. The detailed description is available in [21,22].

A message x is encrypted as: $[x] = (1 + xn)r^n \bmod n^2$, where $r \in \mathbb{Z}_n^*$ is a random number.

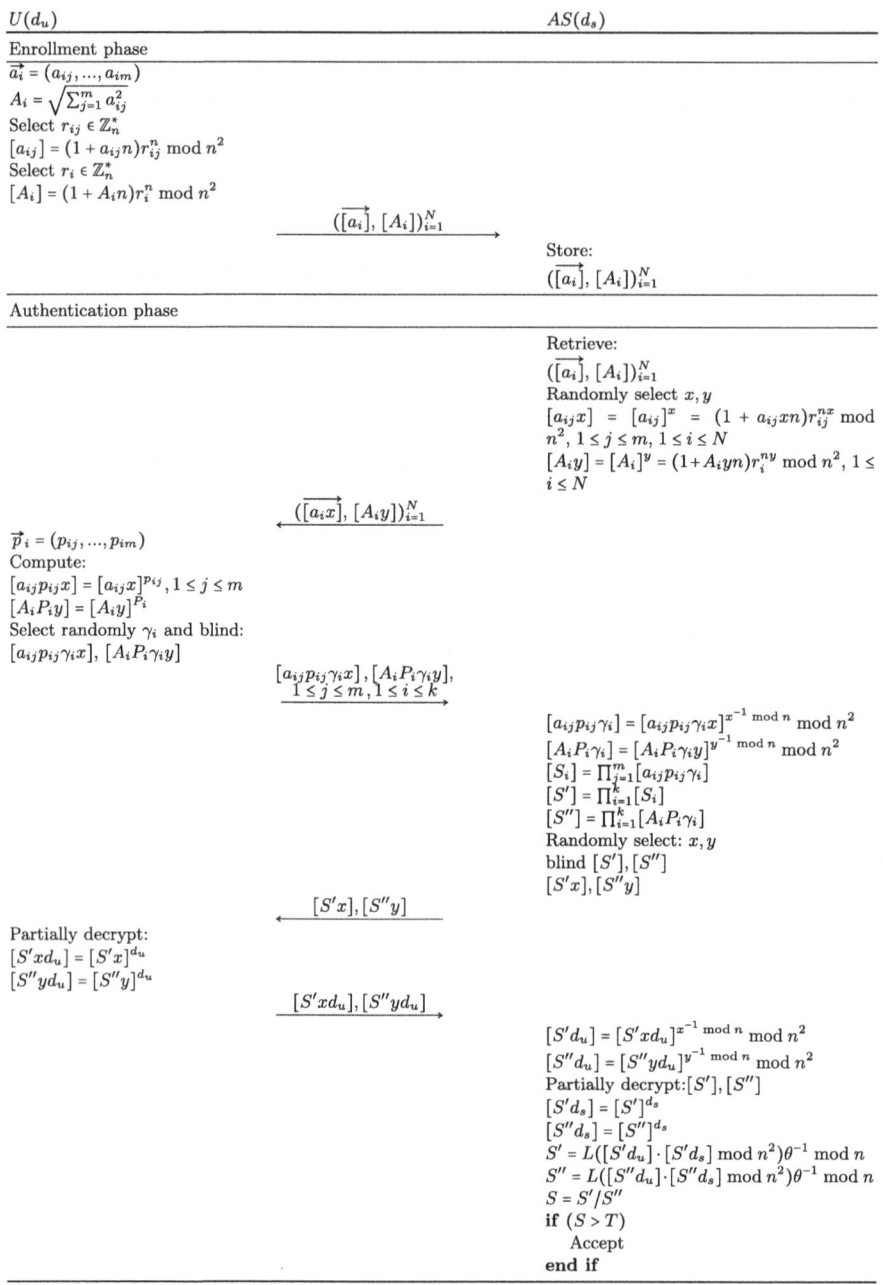

Fig. 1. Authentication phase of proposed protocol

Decryption is only possible when both parties collaborate and partially decrypt a ciphertext. The user partially decrypts as $[x]^{d_u} = ((1 + xn)r^n)^{d_u}$. The authentication server partially decrypts as $[x]^{d_s} = ((1 + xn)r^n)^{d_s}$ and the plaintext is restored by combining the shares as $[x]^{\lambda\beta} = [x]^{d_u} \cdot [x]^{d_s}$ and $x = L([x]^{\lambda\beta} \mod n^2)\theta^{-1} \mod n$, where $L(a) = \frac{a-1}{n}$.

Table 1 presents the notations. The notation $[x]$ represents the encryption of a plaintext x. The Paillier cryptosystem supports the following homomorphic property: $[x_1] \cdot [x_2] = [x_1 + x_2]$. Scalar multiplication can be stated as $[x]^k = [xk]$.

5.2 Enrollment Phase

The enrollment phase is completed in a trusted channel, and both parties trust each other. During the enrollment phase, the user (U) is enrolled in an authentication server (AS), where (AS) stores the encrypted enrollment feature vectors. The user enrollment is completed in a secure channel. The features are extracted from each modality, and reference feature vectors are created. In this phase, the features are sampled $\vec{a}_i = (a_{i1}, ..., a_{im})$ and $A_i = \sqrt{\sum_{j=1}^{m} a_{ij}^2}$ is computed for each activity, similarly as stated in Sect. 4. U selects $r_{ij} \in \mathbb{Z}_n^*$, randomly and encrypts reference feature vectors as $[a_{ij}] = (1 + a_{ij}n)r_{ij}^n \mod n^2$, $1 \leq j \leq m$ and $[A_i] = (1 + A_i n)r_i^n \mod n^2$. U sends the encrypted reference feature vector $\overrightarrow{[a_i]}$ of each activity, and their correspondingly normalized values $[A_i]$ as $(\overrightarrow{[a_i]}, [A_i])_{i=1}^{N}$ to AS for the enrollment, where $\overrightarrow{[a_i]} = ([a_{i1}], ..., [a_{im}])$. AS stores the encrypted reference feature vectors.

5.3 Authentication Phase

At the start of the session, identity verification is done using a first-factor authentication mechanism. Note that continuous authentication is utilized as a second-factor authentication. In this phase, the probe vector is sampled $\vec{p}_i = (p_{i1}, ..., p_{im})$, for the performed activity, and encrypted similarity is computed between an encrypted reference vector $\vec{a}_i$ and the corresponding probe vector $\vec{p}_i$ in the following steps.

Step 1. AS selects two secret random numbers $x, y \in \mathbb{Z}_n$ and blinding each element of all activity vector $\overrightarrow{[a_i]}$ with x as

$$= [a_{ij}]^x = (1 + a_{ij}xn)r_{ij}^{nx} \mod n^2 \qquad (3)$$

and their normalized values $[A_i]$ are blinded with y as

$$= [A_i]^y = (1 + A_i yn)r_i^{ny} \mod n^2 \qquad (4)$$

where each activity contains $(\overrightarrow{[a_i x]} = ([a_{i1}x], ..., [a_{im}x]))$. AS transmits $(\overrightarrow{[a_i x]}, [A_i y])_{i=1}^{N}$ back to U in the beginning of the session.

Step 2. U samples the probe vector $\vec{p}_i = (p_{i1}, ..., p_{im})$ and computes $P_i = \sqrt{\sum_{j=1}^{m} p_{ij}^2}$ for the performed activity. U performs the following computations on the encrypted elements

$$= [a_{ij}x]^{p_{ij}\gamma_i} = (1 + a_{ij}p_{ij}\gamma_i xn) r_{ij}^{p_{ij}\gamma_i xn} \bmod n^2, 1 \le j \le m \quad (5)$$

and

$$= [A_i y]^{P_i \gamma_i} = (1 + A_i P_i \gamma_i yn) r_i^{P_i \gamma_i yn} \bmod n^2 \quad (6)$$

where $\gamma_i \in \mathbb{Z}_n$ is a secret random number; this blinding is canceled out while performing the final division later in step 8.

Step 3. U sends $[a_{ij} p_{ij} x \gamma_i]$, $[A_i P_i \gamma_i y]$, $1 \le j \le m$, $1 \le i \le k$ to AS, without disclosing the information about the performed activity (i).

Step 4. AS computes modular inverse $x^{-1} \bmod n$ and $y^{-1} \bmod n$ and removes the blinding as

$$\begin{aligned}[a_{ij} p_{ij} \gamma_i] &= [a_{ij} p_{ij} \gamma_i x]^{x^{-1}} = (1 + a_{ij} p_{ij} \gamma_i x x^{-1} n) r_{ij}^{p_{ij} \gamma_i x x^{-1} n} \bmod n^2 \\ &= (1 + a_{ij} p_{ij} \gamma_i n) r_{ij}^{p_{ij} \gamma_i n} \bmod n^2, 1 \le j \le m\end{aligned} \quad (7)$$

and

$$\begin{aligned}[A_i P_i \gamma_i] &= [A_i P_i \gamma_i y]^{y^{-1}} = (1 + A_i P_i \gamma_i y y^{-1} n) r_i^{P_i \gamma_i y y^{-1} n} \bmod n^2 \\ &= (1 + A_i P_i \gamma_i n) r_i^{P_i \gamma_i n} \bmod n^2\end{aligned} \quad (8)$$

and homomorphically sums the elements $[a_{ij} p_{ij} \gamma_i], 1 \le j \le m$ as

$$[S_i] = \prod_{j=1}^{m} [a_{ij} p_{ij} \gamma_i] = \prod_{j=1}^{m} (1 + a_{ij} p_{ij} \gamma_i n) r^{p_{ij} \gamma_i n} \bmod n^2 \quad (9)$$

and computes

$$[S_i'] = [A_i P_i \gamma_i] = (1 + A_i P_i \gamma_i n) r_i^{P_i \gamma_i n} \bmod n^2 \quad (10)$$

$[S_i]$ and $[S_i']$ are based on a single activity. To compute the similarity of k activities, AS homomorphically sums the dot products of k activities. The encrypted numerator of Eq. 2 is computed as

$$[S'] = \prod_{i=1}^{k} [S_i] = \prod_{i=1}^{k} \prod_{j=1}^{m} (1 + a_{ij} p_{ij} \gamma_i n) r_{ij}^{p_{ij} \gamma_i n} \bmod n^2 \quad (11)$$

The encrypted denumerator of Eq. 2 is computed as

$$[S''] = \prod_{i=1}^{k} [S_i'] = \prod_{i=1}^{k} (1 + A_i P_i \gamma_i n) r_i^{P_i \gamma_i n} \bmod n^2 \quad (12)$$

To get the similarity score based on k activities, AS has to perform a division between $[S']$ and $[S'']$. Divining two ciphertexts $[S']$ and $[S'']$ is impossible in the

Paillier cryptosystem. AS and U collaborate to perform decryptions $[S']$ and $[S'']$ for the division. AS randomly chooses x, y and blinds $[S']$ and $[S'']$ as

$$[S'x] = [S']^x = \prod_{i=1}^{k}\prod_{j=1}^{m}(1 + a_{ij}p_{ij}\gamma_i xn)r_{ij}^{p_{ij}\gamma_i xn} \bmod n^2 \qquad (13)$$

and

$$[S''y] = [S'']^y = \prod_{i=1}^{k}(1 + A_i P_i \gamma_i yn)r_i^{P_i y \gamma_i n} \bmod n^2 \qquad (14)$$

Step 5. AS sends the blinded $[S'x], [S''y]$ to U for the partial decryption.
Step 6. U partially decrypts $[S'x]$ and $[S''y]$ by his private key share d_u as

$$[S'xd_u] = [S'x]^{d_u} = \prod_{i=1}^{k}\prod_{j=1}^{m}(1 + a_{ij}p_{ij}\gamma_i d_u xn)r_{ij}^{p_{ij}\gamma_i xd_u n} \bmod n^2 \qquad (15)$$

and

$$[S''yd_u] = [S''y]^{d_u} = \prod_{i=1}^{k}(1 + A_i P_i \gamma_i d_u yn)r_i^{P_i y \gamma_i d_u n} \bmod n^2 \qquad (16)$$

Step 7. U sends partially decrypted $[S'xd_u], [S''yd_u]$ to AS.
Step 8. AS computes the modular inverse $x^{-1} \bmod n$ and $y^{-1} \bmod n$ and removes the blinding as

$$\begin{aligned} [S'd_u] = [S'xd_u]^{x^{-1}} &= \prod_{i=1}^{k}\prod_{j=1}^{m}(1 + a_{ij}p_{ij}\gamma_i d_u xx^{-1}n)r_{ij}^{p_{ij}\gamma_i xx^{-1}d_u n} \bmod n^2 \\ &= \prod_{i=1}^{k}\prod_{j=1}^{m}(1 + a_{ij}p_{ij}\gamma_i d_u n)r_{ij}^{p_{ij}\gamma_i d_u n} \bmod n^2 \end{aligned} \qquad (17)$$

and

$$\begin{aligned}[S''d_u] = [S''yd_u]^{y^{-1}} &= \prod_{i=1}^{k}(1 + A_i P_i \gamma_i d_u yy^{-1}n)r_i^{P_i \gamma_i yy^{-1}d_u n} \bmod n^2 \\ &= \prod_{i=1}^{k}(1 + A_i P_i \gamma_i d_u n)r_i^{P_i \gamma_i d_u n} \bmod n^2\end{aligned} \qquad (18)$$

AS already holds $[S']$ and $[S'']$, AS partially decrypts $[S'], [S'']$ by using the private key share d_s

$$[S'd_s] = [S']^{d_s} = \prod_{i=1}^{k}\prod_{j=1}^{m}(1 + a_{ij}p_{ij}\gamma_i d_s n)r_{ij}^{p_{ij}\gamma_i d_s n} \bmod n^2 \qquad (19)$$

and

$$[S''d_s] = [S'']^{d_s} = \prod_{i=1}^{k}(1 + A_i P_i \gamma_i d_s n) r_i^{P_i \gamma_i d_s n} \mod n^2 \quad (20)$$

Now, AS holds the partial decryptions $[S'd_u], [S''d_u], [S'd_s], [S''d_s]$, by combining the shares, AS gets the plaintext as

$$[S'_1]^{\lambda\beta} = [S'd_u] \cdot [S'd_s]$$

$$S' = L([S'_1]^{\lambda\beta} \mod n^2)\theta^{-1} \mod n = \sum_{i=1}^{k}\gamma_i \sum_{j=1}^{m} a_{ij}p_{ij} \quad (21)$$

Similarly,

$$[S'_2]^{\lambda\beta} = [S''d_u] \cdot [S''d_s]$$

$$S'' = L([S'_2]^{\lambda\beta} \mod n^2)\theta^{-1} \mod n = \sum_{i=1}^{k}\gamma_i A_i P_i \quad (22)$$

Finally, AS performs the division as

$$S = \frac{S'}{S''} = \frac{\sum_{i=1}^{k}\gamma_i \sum_{j=1}^{m} a_{ij}p_{ij}}{\sum_{i=1}^{k}\gamma_i A_i P_i} \quad (23)$$

which is in agreement with the Eq. 2.

Due to the blinding factor γ_i imposed by U, AS cannot see S' and S'' but can see only the outcome S. Finally, S is compared to the predefined thresholds, and if $(S > T)$ is true, then the user is accepted; otherwise, authentication is denied. The authentication can be accomplished in two passes, but then we have to reveal the result of each activity, and based on the result, the reference template can be guessed or reconstructed. The proposed protocol takes four passes; the outcome of each activity is homomorphically summed in S' and S'' and is decrypted, which is based on k activities. This makes it hard to guess which activity was performed.

5.4 Security Analysis

The proposed protocol relies on the security assumptions of the Paillier cryptosystem, and the semantic security of the threshold cryptosystem is defined in [21]. The protocol fulfills the following privacy and security requirements.

Theorem 1. The authentication server does not learn stored enrollment vectors based on the assumption that the Paillier cryptosystem is secure, assuming that the decisional composite residuosity assumption (DCRA) problem is computationally intractable.

Proof. The user encrypts the elements of each activity as $[a_{ij}] = (1 + a_{ij}n)r_{ij}^n$ mod n^2 using $(2,2)$-Paillier threshold encryption, which implies that all enrollment vectors $(\overrightarrow{[a_i]}, [A_i])_{i=1}^N$ remain protected. To decrypt a ciphertext, both parties must collaborate (cf. Sect. 5.1). Adversary (AS) can try to determine a_{ij} by brute forcing, but due to the randomness, it is hard to guess. AS can only disclose the enrollment vectors either by correctly guessing d_u or by able to guess $\lambda\beta$.

Theorem 2. The authentication server does not learn probe vectors based on the assumption that the decisional composite residuosity assumption (DCRA) problem is computationally intractable.

During the authentication phase, AS receives encrypted elements $[a_{ij}p_{ij}x\gamma_i]$, $[A_iP_i\gamma_iy]$, $1 \leq j \leq m$, $1 \leq i \leq k$ from U, due the encryption probe vector remain protected from AS. Furthermore, each element is protected by a secret random integer γ_i. This random integer provides protection when the probe has low entropy.

Moreover, revealing the similarity scores of each activity may also reveal information about the enrollment feature vectors. To solve this problem, the proposed protocol makes the authentication decision based on k activities, and AS has no knowledge of which activities are utilized for the authentication and S' and S'' are blinded with $\gamma_i \in \mathbb{Z}_n$ as $S' = \sum_{i=1}^{k} \gamma_i \sum_{j=1}^{m} a_{ij}p_{ij}$ and $S'' = \sum_{i=1}^{k} \gamma_i A_i P_i$ (cf. Eq. 23), so only the final result of k activities is revealed but nothing more, which makes it hard to guess any information about the enrollment vectors.

Theorem 3. A malicious user does not learn the enrollment vectors based on assuming that the decisional composite residuosity assumption (DCRA) problem is computationally intractable.

Proof. A malicious user may deviate from the protocol and request access to the enrollment vectors. The proposed protocol protects the enrollment vectors from the malicious user by using the following mechanisms:

1) Due to $(2,2)$-threshold decryption, U cannot solely decrypt a ciphertext (cf. Sect. 5.1) and cannot see the enrollment feature vectors.
2) During the authentication phase, AS blinds all elements of enrollment feature vectors $(\overrightarrow{[a_i]}, [A_i])_{i=1}^N$, such that the elements in the numerator are blinded with x as $[a_{ij}]^x$, $1 \leq j \leq m$, $1 \leq i \leq N$, and the denumerator elements are blinded with y as $[A_i]^y$, $1 \leq i \leq N$, before sending them to U (cf. Eqs. 3, 4). Adding blindness to the enrollment feature vectors restricts U to follow the protocol because the blindness x, y is removed by AS (cf. Eqs. 7, 8).
3) Similarly, in step 3, AS also sends $[S']$ and $[S'']$ to U blinds S' and S'' with freshly generated x, y (cf. Eqs. 13, 14) and upon receiving message from U, AS removes x, y (cf. Eqs. 17, 18), and deviation from the protocol does not admit a multiplicative inverse.

Hence, U does not get unencrypted enrollment vectors, and any deviation from the protocol in the later stages causes authentication failure.

Theorem 4. During the authentication phase, AS does not learn the type of modality used for authentication.

Proof. During the authentication phase, AS transmits encrypted enrollment vectors of all activities to U, where U can see the index i. In step 2, U transmits $[a_{ij}p_{ij}\gamma_i x]$, $1 \le j \le m$, $[A_i P_i \gamma_i y]$ to AS without the information of i. AS only gets a vector of $[a_{ij}p_{ij}\gamma_i x]$ and $[A_i P_i \gamma_i y]$. Based on ciphertext, AS cannot guess the performed activity. Note that we use only two random numbers (x, y) (cf. Eqs. 3 and 4), x to blind the numerator of each activity and y to blind the denumerator of each activity. As each activity is blinded with the same random numbers, so AS cannot differentiate which activities are exactly performed.

Theorem 5. The proposed protocol resists external attacks based on assuming that the DCRA problem Paillier cryptosystem.

Proof. We assume the external adversary controls the public channel. The external adversary cannot break the ciphertext but can replay the transmitted messages. To solve such a problem, we include a challenge-response mechanism with freshly generated random numbers (x, y, γ_i) for each transmission (cf. Eqs. 3, 4, 5, 6, 13, 14). During the authentication phase of the proposed protocol, AS generates x, y twice and blinds enrollment vectors and aggregated scores before sending them to U. Upon receiving messages from U, AS removes the random numbers (cf. Eqs. 7, 8, 17, 18), which implies that any previously transmitted message that is replayed by the adversary gives a completely different result as stated above that old messages do not admit a multiplicative inverse, this causes a failure in the authentication (Table 2).

6 Performance Evaluation

This section analyzes the communication cost of the proposed protocol. Table 4 shows the security comparison of the proposed protocol.

Table 2. Security comparison

Protocol	Cryptosystem (s)	Adversarial model	Data protection	Activity protection	External adversaries
[7]	DGK HE+ Symmetric encryption+ DGK-PPCP	Honest client, semi-honest server	Yes	No	No
[23]	Garbled circuits+ DGK-PPCP	Honest client, semi-honest server	Yes	No	No
[15]	Paillier+ Symmetric encryption	Malicious client, semi-honest server	Insecure	No	No
[17]	Paillier threshold cryptosystem	Semi-honest server semi-honest client	Yes	Yes	No
Proposed protocol	Paillier threshold cryptosystem	Malicious client, semi-honest server, external adversaries	Yes	Yes	Yes

6.1 Communication Cost

The proposed protocol has a very low communication cost. The first pass transmits feature vectors $(\overrightarrow{[a_i]}, [A_i])_{i=1}^{N}$ to U only once for k activities. The second pass transmits $km + k$ ciphertexts to AS. After k activities, AS and U perform interaction and exchange four ciphertexts. To make an authentication decision based on K activities, the proposed protocol transmits $(N \times m + N + k \times m + k + 4)$ encryptions. Table 4 presents the cost comparison of the proposed protocol.

In comparison to the literature, the protocols presented in [7,14] complete authentication by utilizing Damgård et al. [10,11], privacy-preserving greater than comparison protocol for their computation, which makes it impractical in the domain of continuous authentication. Wei et al. [15] protocol takes three rounds to compute the similarity scores of one activity. In each round, they transmit m encrypted elements; in total, they transmit $3 \times m$ encryption for one activity; this protocol makes $3 \times k \times m$ passes transmissions for k activities, which causes communication overhead.

Domingo-Ferrer et al. [4] protocol takes two rounds of communication to compute the intersection between two sets, and each round transmits m ciphertexts. Shahandashti et al. [6] takes two rounds to complete the authentication decision, and each round transmits m ciphertexts; this protocol makes $2 \times k \times m$ passes transmissions for k activities, which causes communication overhead.

Baig et al. [17] proposed two protocols: the first protocol transmits $(N \times m+7)$, and the second protocol transmits $(N \times m + k + 7)$ ciphertexts. The proposed protocol has a very efficient communication cost compared to the existing protocols [4,6,7,14,15]. Note that the communication cost plays a very important role in the domain of continuous authentication.

6.2 Biometric Evaluation

To evaluate the biometric performance of the proposed protocol, we used two datasets: A swipe gesture dataset [18][1] and a keystroke dynamics dataset [24][2]

Both datasets contain l samples of different participants; in both cases, we randomly select a sample from l samples and make it a template. In the case of swipe gestures, two templates are created, a horizontal and a vertical. In the case of keystroke dynamics, only one template is created. The templates are encrypted using the Paillier cryptosystem by following the steps of the enrollment phase, stated in Sect. 5.2. The performance of the proposed protocols is determined by computing the false non-match rate (FNMR), false match rate (FMR), and equal error rate (EER). To compute FNMR, we compute the similarity between the encrypted templates and other $l - 1$ samples. Each swipe gesture sample consists of a vector of 15 elements, and each keystroke sample contains a vector of 31 elements. To determine FMR, we chose a few samples from each user, constructed imposter samples for each user, and computed the similarity between the template and the imposter samples.

---

[1] Available at https://www.ms.sapientia.ro/~manyi/bioident/dataset1.arff.
[2] Available at https://www.cs.cmu.edu/~keystroke/.

Table 3. Biometric performance of swipe gesture and keystroke

<table>
<tr><td colspan="4">(a) Swipe gesture</td><td colspan="4">(b) Keystroke dynamics</td></tr>
<tr><td>T</td><td>FNMR</td><td>FMR</td><td>EER</td><td>T</td><td>FNMR</td><td>FMR</td><td>EER</td></tr>
<tr><td>0.95</td><td>0.397</td><td>0.100</td><td>0.249</td><td>0.95</td><td>0.564</td><td>0.062</td><td>0.313</td></tr>
<tr><td>0.94</td><td>0.364</td><td>0.115</td><td>0.240</td><td>0.94</td><td>0.500</td><td>0.092</td><td>0.296</td></tr>
<tr><td>0.93</td><td>0.331</td><td>0.133</td><td>0.232</td><td>0.93</td><td>0.431</td><td>0.115</td><td>0.273</td></tr>
<tr><td>0.92</td><td>0.306</td><td>0.165</td><td>0.236</td><td>0.92</td><td>0.367</td><td>0.171</td><td>0.269</td></tr>
<tr><td>0.91</td><td>0.269</td><td>0.183</td><td>0.226</td><td>0.91</td><td>0.281</td><td>0.208</td><td>0.245</td></tr>
<tr><td>0.90</td><td>0.242</td><td>0.198</td><td>0.220</td><td>0.90</td><td>0.239</td><td>0.258</td><td>0.249</td></tr>
<tr><td>0.89</td><td>0.236</td><td>0.221</td><td>0.228</td><td>0.89</td><td>0.192</td><td>0.319</td><td>0.256</td></tr>
<tr><td>0.88</td><td>0.219</td><td>0.233</td><td>0.226</td><td>0.88</td><td>0.161</td><td>0.369</td><td>0.265</td></tr>
<tr><td>0.87</td><td>0.206</td><td>0.246</td><td>0.226</td><td>0.87</td><td>0.150</td><td>0.419</td><td>0.285</td></tr>
<tr><td>0.86</td><td>0.194</td><td>0.275</td><td>0.235</td><td>0.86</td><td>0.128</td><td>0.444</td><td>0.286</td></tr>
<tr><td>0.85</td><td>0.181</td><td>0.306</td><td>0.243</td><td>0.85</td><td>0.111</td><td>0.483</td><td>0.297</td></tr>
</table>

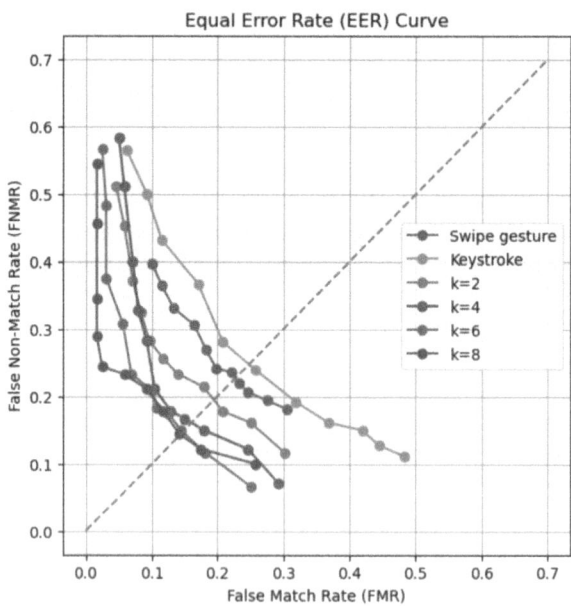

Fig. 2. Biometric performance of the proposed protocol

Table 4. Biometric performance on combined data

T	k = 2 FNMR	FMR	EER	k = 4 FNMR	FMR	EER	k = 6 FNMR	FMR	EER	k = 8 FNMR	FMR	EER
0.95	0.511	0.046	0.279	0.583	0.050	0.317	0.567	0.025	0.296	0.544	0.017	0.281
0.94	0.453	0.058	0.256	0.511	0.058	0.285	0.483	0.031	0.257	0.456	0.017	0.237
0.93	0.372	0.071	0.222	0.400	0.071	0.236	0.375	0.031	0.203	0.344	0.017	0.181
0.92	0.325	0.083	0.204	0.328	0.079	0.204	0.308	0.056	0.182	0.289	0.017	0.153
0.91	0.283	0.096	0.190	0.283	0.092	0.188	0.233	0.069	0.151	0.244	0.025	0.135
0.90	0.256	0.117	0.187	0.211	0.104	0.158	0.208	0.100	0.154	0.233	0.058	0.146
0.89	0.233	0.14	0.187	0.178	0.129	0.154	0.183	0.106	0.145	0.211	0.092	0.152
0.88	0.214	0.179	0.197	0.167	0.150	0.159	0.175	0.125	0.150	0.178	0.117	0.148
0.87	0.178	0.208	0.193	0.150	0.179	0.165	0.150	0.144	0.147	0.144	0.142	0.143
0.86	0.161	0.25	0.206	0.122	0.246	0.184	0.117	0.181	0.149	0.122	0.175	0.149
0.85	0.117	0.302	0.210	0.072	0.292	0.182	0.067	0.250	0.159	0.100	0.258	0.179

To evaluate the performance of the proposed protocol on single and multimodal data, we considered the following authentication scenarios and performed the biometric evaluation as follows:

Scenario 1 (k = 1). We compute the similarity based on a single activity $k = 1$; in this scenario, the similarity of swipe gesture and keystroke is determined individually. Table 3a presents the biometric performance on a swipe-gesture dataset, and Table 3b presents the biometric performance on a keystroke dataset. Note that this similarity is according to the original cosine similarity of Eq. 1.

Further, we tested the extended similarity of Eq. 2, and made the following multimodal authentication scenarios

Scenario 2 (k = 2). In this scenario, the similarity is determined based on 2 activities- we used 1 swipe gesture with 1 keystroke pattern for authentication.

Scenario 3 (k = 4). In this scenario, the similarity is determined based on 4 activities- we used 2 swipe gestures and 2 keystroke patterns for authentication.

Scenario 4 (k = 6). In this scenario, the similarity is determined based on 6 activities- we used 3 swipe gestures and 3 keystroke patterns for authentication.

Scenario 5 (k = 8). In this scenario, the similarity is determined based on 8 activities- we used 4 swipe gestures and 4 keystroke patterns for authentication.

We computed the numerator and denominator separately, then the dot products of both vectors are summed in the numerator, and their corresponding normalized values are summed in the denominator as stated in the authentication phase of the proposed protocol Fig. 1. Table 4 and Fig. 2 present the biometric performance of the proposed protocol.

To the best of our knowledge, this work is the first to present a multimodal privacy-preserving continuous authentication protocol. By comparing the results, we can see that our extended approach performs better than the original cosine similarity. Moreover, as U and AS interact after k activities, this results in low communication costs.

Besides the biometric performance, we measured the running time of the proposed protocol on Intel(R) Core(TM) 11th Gen Intel(R) Core(TM) i5-1145G7 @ 2.60 GHz 1.50 GHz on Python 3.11; we use the 1050-bit key-size to determine the running time of the proposed protocol. We consider the continuous authentication using ($k = 2, 4, 6, 8$), as stated above. The running time of the proposed protocol is presented in Fig. 3.

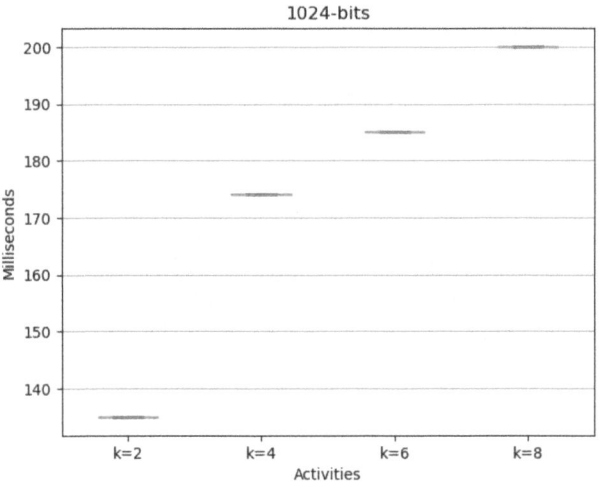

Fig. 3. Running time of proposed protocol

7 Conclusions and Future Work

In this paper, we have proposed a secure and privacy-preserving protocol that enables multimodal continuous authentication. The proposed protocol has efficient communication and computation costs. The biometric evaluation of the proposed protocol on two public datasets has proved that the proposed protocol can be used to achieve continuous authentication using a single modality as well as a combination of multiple modalities without any modifications. Further, the proposed protocol provides security in the presence of malicious user, semi-honest authentication server, and external adversaries.

Our future work will consider the malicious authentication server, who can deviate from the protocol to learn the user activities. Moreover, we will also focus on making the final comparison in a privacy-preserving way.

Acknowledgement. This work has been funded by the Leveraging Security and Privacy Technologies for Inclusive eID and Access Control Services (IncluDe) project. The include project has received funding from the Research council of Norway from 2024–2027 under project number 349943. This work has also been co-funded by the project Center for Cyber and Information Security of NTNU-IIK.

References

1. Baig, A.F., Eskeland, S.: Security, privacy, and usability in continuous authentication: A survey. Sensors **21**(17), 5967 (2021)
2. GDPR, Processing of special categories of personal data (2021). https://gdpr-info.eu/art-9-gdpr/. Accessed 03 Mar 2023
3. Safa, N.A., Safavi-Naini, R., Shahandashti, S.F.: Privacy-preserving implicit authentication. In: IFIP International Information Security Conference, pp. 471–484. Springer (2014)
4. Domingo-Ferrer, J., Wu, Q., Blanco-Justicia, A.: Flexible and robust privacy-preserving implicit authentication. In: IFIP International Information Security and Privacy Conference, pp. 18–34. Springer (2015)
5. Eskeland, S.: Cryptanalysis of a privacy-preserving authentication scheme based on private set intersection. J. Math. Cryptol. **18**(1), 20230032 (2024)
6. Shahandashti, S.F., Safavi-Naini, R., Safa, N.A.: Reconciling user privacy and implicit authentication for mobile devices. Comput. Secur. **53**, 215–233 (2015)
7. Govindarajan, S., Gasti, P., Balagani, K.S.: Secure privacy-preserving protocols for outsourcing continuous authentication of smartphone users with touch data. In: 2013 IEEE Sixth International Conference on Biometrics: Theory, Applications and Systems (BTAS), pp. 1–8. IEEE (2013)
8. Damgård, I., Geisler, M., Krøigard, M.: Homomorphic encryption and secure comparison. Int. J. Appl. Cryptography **1**(1), 22–31 (2008)
9. Erkin, Z., Franz, M., Guajardo, J., Katzenbeisser, S., Lagendijk, I., Toft, T.: Privacy-preserving face recognition. In: International Symposium on Privacy Enhancing Technologies Symposium, pp. 235–253. Springer (2009)
10. Damgård, I., Geisler, M., Krøigaard, M.: Efficient and secure comparison for on-line auctions. In: Australasian conference on information security and privacy, pp. 416–430. Springer (2007)
11. Damgård, I., Geisler, M., Krøigard, M.: A correction to Efficient and secure comparison for on-line auctions. Int. J. Appl. Cryptography **1**(4), 323–324 (2009)
12. Sitová, Z., Šeděnka, J., Yang, Q., Peng, G., Zhou, G., Gasti, P., Balagani, K.S.: Hmog: new behavioral biometric features for continuous authentication of smartphone users. IEEE Trans. Inf. Forensics Secur. **11**(5), 877–892 (2015)
13. Juels, A., Wattenberg, M.: A fuzzy commitment scheme. In: Proceedings of the 6th ACM Conference on Computer and Communications Security, pp. 28–36 (1999)

14. Balagani, K.S., Gasti, P., Elliott, A., Richardson, A., O'Neal, M.: The impact of application context on privacy and performance of keystroke authentication systems. J. Comput. Secur. **26**(4), 543–556 (2018)
15. Wei, F., Vijayakumar, P., Kumar, N., Zhang, R., Cheng, Q.: Privacy-preserving implicit authentication protocol using cosine similarity for internet of things. IEEE Internet Things J. **8**(7), 5599–5606 (2020)
16. Eskeland, S., Baig, A.F.: Cryptanalysis of a privacy-preserving behavior-oriented authentication scheme. In: Proceedings of the 19th International Conference on Security and Cryptography - SECRYPT 2022, INSTICC. SciTePress, pp. 299–304 (2022)
17. Baig, A.F., Eskeland, S., Yang, B.: Privacy-preserving continuous authentication using behavioral biometrics. Int. J. Inf. Secur., 15 (2023)
18. Antal, M., Bokor, Z., Szabó, L.Z.: Information revealed from scrolling interactions on mobile devices. Pattern Recogn. Lett. **56**, 7–13 (2015)
19. Killourhy, K., Maxion, R.: Free vs. Transcribed Text for Keystroke-Dynamics Evaluations
20. Baig, A.F., Eskeland, S., Yang, B.: Novel and efficient privacy-preserving continuous authentication. Cryptography **8**(1), 3 (2024)
21. Fouque, P.-A., Poupard, G., Stern, J.: Sharing decryption in the context of voting or lotteries. In: Financial Cryptography: 4th International Conference, FC: Anguilla, British West Indies, February 20–24, 2000 Proceedings 4, pp. 90–104. Springer (2000)
22. Veugen, T., Attema, T., Spini, G.: An implementation of the paillier crypto system with threshold decryption without a trusted dealer. Cryptology ePrint Archive (2019)
23. Šeděnka, J., Govindarajan, S., Gasti, P., Balagani, K.S.: Secure outsourced biometric authentication with performance evaluation on smartphones. IEEE Trans. Inf. Forensics Secur. **10**(2), 384–396 (2014)
24. Killourhy, K.S., Maxion, R.A.: Free vs. transcribed text for keystroke-dynamics evaluations. In: Proceedings of the 2012 Workshop on Learning from Authoritative Security Experiment Results, pp. 1–8 (2012)

Cyber Security in Healthcare Systems: A Review of Tools and Attack Mitigation Techniques

Kousik Barik[1], Sanjay Misra[2], and Sabarathinam Chockalingam[3]([✉])

[1] Department of Computer Science, University of Alcala, Madrid, Spain
Kousik.Kousik@edu.uah.es
[2] Department of Applied Data Science, Institute for Energy Technology, Halden, Norway
Sanjay.Misra@ife.no
[3] Department of Risk and Security, Institute for Energy Technology, Halden, Norway
Sabarathinam.Chockalingam@ife.no

Abstract. In recent years, healthcare, and financial sectors have experienced a significant increase in cyber-attacks. The healthcare sector, in particular, has been a major target due to its inadequate security measures and the sensitivity of its data. This vulnerability, despite its critical impact on patient services and hospital reputation, has not received the necessary priority in terms of cyber security. The potential consequences, including data breaches, patient safety risks, and reputational damage to the healthcare organization, are severe and should cause immediate concern. This study aims to explore the impact of cyber security on healthcare systems. We employed a Systematic Literature Review (SLR) methodology, and 43 existing studies were analyzed. This study highlights the significance of cyber security in healthcare systems and cyber security tools employed in healthcare. It also outlines the existing cyber-attacks and mitigation strategies in healthcare settings. Furthermore, we highlight the research gaps in cyber security of healthcare systems, providing a foundation for future research in this area.

Keywords: Attacks · Cyber security · Healthcare · Mitigation strategies · Tools

1 Introduction

Cyber security protects computer systems and networks from unauthorized access, data theft, and service disruptions. Ensuring the security of digital data is a top priority for every organization. The healthcare industry has become a prime target for cybercrime. Healthcare organizations are increasingly adopting emerging technologies such as the Internet of Things (IoT), Artificial Intelligence (AI), and blockchain [1]. These technologies have the potential to revolutionize healthcare, by optimizing operations and achieving new objectives. However, this positive outlook on technological advancement also highlights the need for strong cyber security measures, which are particularly crucial for the future of healthcare. In medical institutions, the importance of cyber security has reached unprecedented levels. Health departments, healthcare consultancies, and primary healthcare practices are especially vulnerable to data theft, identity theft, and unauthorized system breaches caused by various cyber-attacks [2]. To mitigate these risks, it is essential to implement comprehensive security measures that address people, processes, and technology. For instance, strong authentication methods combined with personalized employee training can reduce the likelihood of a breach. Healthcare organizations face increasing exposure to cyber threats, with attackers often exploiting vulnerabilities in the supply chain network [3]. Due to their dependence on various suppliers and third-party providers, these organizations manage complex systems that involve constant exchange of large volumes of data. Healthcare professionals are also responsible for securing this data and protecting patients and organizations [4]. Over the years, numerous health information data breaches have occurred, predominantly due to hacking. One notable incident involved a ransomware attack on the University of Vermont Health Network, resulting in approximately 50 million US dollars in expenses [5].

An inherent challenge in cyber security is that attackers consistently outplay organizations. Their goal is to exploit vulnerabilities that organizations are likely to overlook [6]. As attackers rapidly develop new techniques, cyber security professionals must remain vigilant to prevent, identify, detect and respond to attacks. To effectively implement this reactive approach, periodic updates and modifications are required [7]. The susceptibility to cybercrime grows with the increasing technological integration in the healthcare industry. Two different categories of threats exist: external and inside threat. External cybercriminals infiltrate healthcare records systems to acquire sensitive information for financial gain, such as exploiting patients' confidential data to file fraudulent insurance claims [8]. External threat can also involve attackers demanding ransomware payments to restore access to patient records. Advanced malware, phishing techniques, DDoS attacks and other malicious software designed to steal user login credentials can compromise entire systems. Training staff to recognize and respond to coordinated phishing attempts is important in preventing such attacks [9].

Technological advances have greatly improved patient care, data retrieval, and communication between patients and staff through interconnected systems in medical institutions. However, these advances also introduce a certain level of risk [10]. Threat actors are increasingly targeting the healthcare industry, mainly due to sensitive personal and financial information. The importance of cyber security in healthcare cannot be overstated, as threat actors continuously find vulnerabilities in healthcare systems. The pandemic has further exposed numerous healthcare facilities, research centers, and hospitals to cyber threats, highlighting the need for adopting a robust cyber security strategy [11]. The emergence of digital transformation has made the healthcare sector more vulnerable to cyber threats, as key players increasingly adopt technologies, such as mobile applications and public cloud services. Security breaches affecting confidential patient data present a substantial and immediate threat to critical healthcare services [12].

Patient information is accessible to internal employees of healthcare organizations. The misuse of stolen data by attackers can take various forms. Attackers can manipulate this information to commit identity theft or conduct fraudulent transactions. They can also infiltrate computer systems, install malware, or steal the system's login credentials [13]. A common phishing technique involving soliciting login credentials through emails that appear to be legitimate. Securing Electronic Health Records (EHR) and Personal Health Information (PHI) is of essential for building patient trust during a interactions with healthcare professionals [14]. The primary distinction is that an EHR is a record system, while PHI refers to the information contained within that record. The increasing prevalence of cyber threats is expected to result in more stringent regulations, strengthening the need for healthcare organizations to protect against cyber threats [15]. The main contributions of this study are as follows:

- To identify key cyber security applications in healthcare systems.
- To identify security tools for enhancing cyber security in healthcare organizations.
- To determine mitigation strategies of addressing cyber threats in healthcare organizations.
- To highlight open issues of cyber security in healthcare systems.

The comprehensive selection of research papers is crucial for identifying relevant information on the chosen topic. This study employs a Preferred Reporting Items for Systematic Reviews and Meta-Analyses (PRISMA) guidelines, a comprehensive approach that begins with an initial collection of articles identified through targeted keyword searches in specialized scientific databases. The authors conducted their research based on selection criteria for cyber security applications in healthcare, tools, mitigation strategies, and open challenges. Initially, 345 articles were identified using the search string provided in Table 1, retrieving relevant studies from six different scientific databases including: ACM Digital Library, IEEE Xplore, Scopus, ScienceDirect, SpringerLink, and Wiley. After reviewing the titles and abstracts, 126 studies were selected. After the full-text screening, we selected studies 43 studies for in-depth analysis. Figure 1 presents a flow diagram illustrating the methodology of our study selection process.

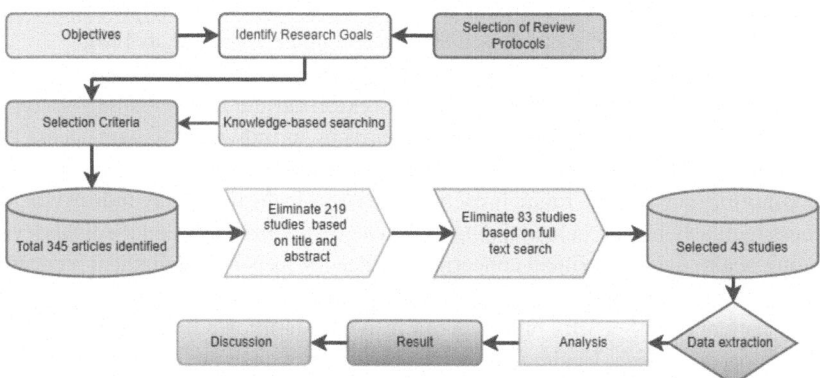

Fig. 1. Research methodology for data extraction

The remainder of the is structured as follows: Sect. 2 discusses application of cyber security in healthcare organizations. Section 3 presents security tools used for cyber security in healthcare systems. Section 4 highlights cyber-attacks and mitigation strategies in healthcare systems. Section 5 provides a discussion of open challenges, and future research directions. Finally, Sect. 6 presents conclusions of this study.

Table 1. Search string and search results.

Search String: (("Cybersecurity Tools" OR "Attack Mitigation") AND ("Healthcare"))		
Scientific Database	Number of Papers Found	Filters
IEEE Xplore	12	Conferences and Journals
Scopus	23	
Science Direct	134	
SpringerLink	115	Article, Research Article, Conference Paper
ACM Digital Library	26	Research Article
Wiley	35	Journals
Total	345	

2 Applications of Cyber Security in Healthcare Systems

Healthcare organizations are highly susceptible to cyber-attacks due to vast amount of data they hold, which threat actors target for financial gain and intelligence purpose. In addition, patient's secure health record and personal information for critical medical examination and invention are highly sensitive and confidential [16]. Hospitals rely on complex technical infrastructures that use cyber security measures to manage large volumes of data and ensure operational requirements are met. Magnetic Resonance Imaging (MRI) machines are often connected to multiple terminals, allowing technicians to adjust MRI views. However, these devices can serve as possible entry points for attempting to access information in systems connected through the intranet. In some cases, confidential information may be only partially encrypted or left unprotected. Clinicians often use pseudonymization to anonymize diseases or healthcare procedures during patient interactions [5]. Medical professionals also employ anonymization when handling data for statistical analysis or as a part of a strategic effort to improve specific services [17]. Healthcare organizations must implement robust security mechanisms to minimize the possibility of email-based attacks and other cyber threats [18].

Due to the storage of sensitive data and the provision of high-quality patient services, healthcare systems are particularly vulnerable to extortion attempts. Phishing is a typical cyber-attack where attackers target a trusted company or individual to gain access [19]. Email systems, including links to fraudulent websites in messages, are frequently used entry points for such attacks. Email breaches pose a risk in the healthcare industry, as staff members regularly handle personal data [20]. The distinction between medical devices managing health data is a critical concern for attackers, as personal medical records are strictly regulated. These regulations enforce additional measures to ensure the confidentiality of patient data. Security breaches can result in significant financial liabilities for healthcare organizations. Healthcare sector must be proficient and prepared to take the required steps to protect their health applications. The information collected in healthcare systems is highly sensitive, and if compromised can become a substantial liability [21]. Healthcare organizations are prime targets for attackers aiming to steal valuable information by exploiting weaknesses in security protocols. Medical professionals must be competent in managing and efficiently using current technologies. Personnel are especially vulnerable to phishing and spoofing attacks. Furthermore, employees should be provided with information about the reporting system for suspicious behavior, further strengthening their capabilities to respond to threats [22]. Training staff on the secure and efficient usage of technology, while protecting their network, should be a top priority [23]. Table 2 provides a summary of cyber security applications used in healthcare systems.

Table 2. Cyber security application in healthcare systems

S. No	References	Applications	Description
1	[24, 25]	Healthcare Data Protection	Cyber security enhances the identification, prevention, detection, analysis, and prompt response to cyber-attacks. It improves operational efficiency and strengthens information technology security within organizations
2	[26, 27]	Protection of Medical Equipment	Attackers can exploit connected medical devices to disrupt healthcare organizations. Whether data breaches occur inadvertently or intentionally, it is the responsibility of all personnel to ensure effective cyber security management. Continued and tailored cyber security training/education to healthcare professionals is essential for advancing cyber security
3	[28, 29]	Extended Patient Service	The primary goal of the healthcare industry has been to deliver high-quality care to patients. The modern healthcare heavily relies on technological advancements, which is beneficial. However, it also expands attack surface and increase risks. Medical manufacturers should evaluate the cyber threats to products and technology utilized in hospitals and other healthcare organizations. Because of limited financial resources, smaller organizations often find themselves more vulnerable, as attackers recognize that their security standards may be easier to compromise. A thorough understanding of the key elements of healthcare data security will improve the future security of organizations and their patients
4	[30, 31]	Risk Assessment	A risk analysis must be performed periodically, and security measures should be implemented to mitigate cyber threats in healthcare. Healthcare organizations should perform periodic penetration testing, vulnerability analysis, and audits to analyze the effectiveness of their security systems

(continued)

Table 2. (*continued*)

S. No	References	Applications	Description
5	[32, 33]	Attack Prevention	Healthcare cyber security aims to prevent unauthorized access, use, and disclosure of patient information while ensuring the confidentiality and integrity of patient information
6	[34, 35]	Network Systems	Ensuring the security of healthcare communications transmitted across different devices is crucial. It allows doctors and other associates to retrieve patients' data efficiently. However, it is equally important to address vulnerabilities in data security that could be exploited by malware. The significant technical advancements in data collection methods have greatly enhanced their capacity to store and record information on cloud-hosted servers
7	[36, 37]	Healthcare Fraud	Vigilance in cyber security is essential for healthcare organizations to prevent legal matters, fraud, and damage to brand reputation resulting from disclosure of sensitive patient data. It is crucial to implement appropriate and robust security measures in addition to tailored cyber security training for all staff members to prepare them to understand the significance of cyber security. Adversaries often exploit the credentials of authorized users to illegally access organizational systems. It is critical to limit access to these systems enforcing strict and logical access rules will improve organization's overall security
8	[38, 39]	Managing Daily Operations	Technologies and standards for information security and cyber security are important. Healthcare organizations can protect their systems and day-to-day activities against attackers by implementing cost-effective security tools and initiatives to monitor and prevent breaches. Hospital systems must regularly provide software updates through a standard procedure to ensure the latest versions are installed

(*continued*)

Table 2. (*continued*)

S. No	References	Applications	Description
9	[40, 41]	Trusted Connectivity	Many healthcare organizations adopt cloud-based storage solution, as this technology enhances devices' secured connection and usefulness for easy access
10	[42, 43]	Enhancing Outcomes	Implementing cyber security standards improves both the accessibility and efficiency of providing patient care, thereby enhancing healthcare service quality. As overwhelmed personnel and IT teams manage changing priorities, fundamental cyber security standards can easily be overlooked, putting medical data and, increasingly, patient well-being at risk. Historically, cybercriminals have seen the healthcare industry as a highly appealing target. Researchers are investigating novel methods to strengthen healthcare cyber security, including protecting sensitive patient data and implementing strict policies to prevent any instances of system unavailability that may interfere with patient care

3 Tools of Cyber Security in Healthcare Systems

The field of healthcare cyber security protects healthcare records, patient information, and assets from illegal access, disclosure, and misuse. With technical advancement, the number of possible digital entry points for cybercrime grows exponentially. Integrating AI, IoT, and cloud computing has significantly expanded the scope of possible uses in the domain of patient monitoring [44]. The increasing number of healthcare organizations outsourcing various service delivery elements to third-party supplier's increases security concerns. For example, organizations may employ the services of a call center to provide patient support, along with other service providers and external parties [45]. Each new third-party organization relationship introduces additional risks and expands their attack surface for protected health data. Like many other industries, healthcare organizations rely on interconnected systems to improve efficiency and access to information [46]. This growing interconnectedness furthermore carries a substantial risk of cyber-attacks.

Healthcare businesses must establish a comprehensive cyber security policy to protect their computer infrastructure from attacks [47]. This policy encompasses more than protecting hospital personal computers [47]. A strategy approach that recognizes the urgent need to protect information technology, building systems, and clinical equipment is essential. However, service providers tend to overlook the focus on cyber security when implementing new systems. Healthcare executives should understand the significance of cyber security and gather the knowledge necessary to implement it effectively [48].

Given the technological complexity and dependence on mobile devices in healthcare, organizations should employ encryption techniques and other related security measures [49]. Antivirus software should be updated regularly to monitor and secure network activities. The healthcare cyber security workforce consists of professionals in the health information management sector. Health information management provides patient information precision, security, and confidentiality [50]. As electronic health records and digital healthcare systems become more prevalent in hospitals, professionals should efficiently manage and protect this digital data. Backups are a critical component of any security response and recovery plan. Health information, often protected under the HIPPA (Health Insurance Portability and Accountability Act), is confidential and targeted by hostile threats. [51]. Most healthcare organizations have a clear physical access protocols for hospital systems. They have WiFi and typically have accessible ports for connecting medical devices. In addition, outdated technologies and devices with unnecessary internet integration increase the probability of exposure [52]. Cybercriminals can exploit these entry points to access sensitive data. The swift processing of digital information has led to influential advances in healthcare [53]. The improvement in automation and interoperability has thus amplified the vulnerability to cyber disruptions.

Operational technologies additionally challenge achieving standards using IoT. The integration of numerous product categories brings new cyber security issues [54]. Hence, new forms of governance are necessary to manage the emerging challenges of the digital environment effectively. Most of the data privacy leakage in healthcare is driven by internal staff abuse and unauthorized exposure. Cyber security is not a primary concern for most hospital staff in an overwhelmed organization. Concerning fundamental cyber security, the healthcare sector should catch up with more advanced businesses like banking and manufacturing, often including data protection in their infrastructure. The task is challenging, considering the potentially profitable nature of healthcare breaches for attackers [55].

Medical Internet of Things (IoMT) collects mobile devices and related systems to store patient information. Apart from confidential health data, there is also valuable institutional property valued by key stakeholders that is vulnerable to cyber threat [56]. With the rising prevalence of healthcare cybercrime and the demanding medical records expenses, there is a growing allocation of funds towards rectifying the damage resulting from the loss of this vital medical information. Equally important is the demand for fundamental healthcare personnel to have cyber security skills [57]. Healthcare professionals are most often targeted compared to senior-level employees, doctors, and administrative staff. Attackers possess intelligent skills and are experienced at capitalizing on human vulnerability inside medical organizations [58]. Cybercriminals conduct periodic analyses to determine the precise targets for their attacks, exploit doctors pressed for time, keep inherent interests, and have an enduring desire to enhance welfare. Recent advancements in AI, blockchain, and quantum computing are significantly enhancing healthcare cyber security by strengthening the protection of sensitive medical data and infrastructure against increasingly complex cyber threats. AI is essential in cyber security, as it processes vast amounts of data and identifies patterns humans may miss [59]. In healthcare, AI's role in cyber security focuses on early threat detection, real-time monitoring, and automated responses to cyber incidents. Blockchain technology provides a decentralized, immutable ledger system that enhances the security and integrity of healthcare data. Quantum computing, an emerging technology, has the potential both to improve and to challenge healthcare cyber security [60]. The tools of cyber security in healthcare organizations are outlined in Fig. 2.

Fig. 2. Cyber security tools in healthcare

4 Threats and Mitigation of Cyber-Attacks in Healthcare Systems

Healthcare businesses encounter a significant problem in cyber security, as they face the weaknesses and possible abuse of patient data. Healthcare information, such as clinical records and financial details, may aid in creating a comprehensive individual biography [61]. The usefulness of the data is enhanced when a transaction's completion has been confirmed. Before the patient's awareness of the illegal disclosure of their data, the sale of these documents on the dark web may lead to their repeated use [62]. The health industry is extremely susceptible to cyber-attacks that can produce catastrophic public health and security consequences [63]. Multiple cyber security challenges impact the healthcare sector. These include DDoS attacks, which limit healthcare organizations' capability to provide patient service and ransomware attacks. Cyber-attacks can have far-reaching consequences on the healthcare industry beyond financial losses and privacy violations. Ransomware attacks substantially risk hospitals since compromising patient data may threaten lives. Table 3 demonstrates the common healthcare cyber-attacks.

Risk is the likelihood of damage if an adversary manipulates a vulnerability in the system. Risk mitigation is necessary to minimize such damage. It consists of two methods: risk reduction and risk avoidance. The mitigation methods include proactive

Table 3. Healthcare cyber security - common attack types

S. No	Ref. No	Attacks	Description
1	[64]	DDoS	It deliberately inundates a specific computer with fraudulent connection requests to make it inoperable. DDoS floods network and disrupts or impairs critical services, often restricting access to vital information and making medical services unavailable
2	[65]	Ransomware	This malware affects nonfunctioning systems, encrypts data, and especially limits patient services, emphasizing the critical significance of cyber security in healthcare administration. The installation of the malware is specific, and it often multiplies to machines through phishing emails, which may include hostile files or links
3	[66]	Data breach	While data breaches may not always result from threats, they can happen if malware, hacked organizations, or internal threats are involved. Data encryption and backup are recommended
4	[67]	User awareness	Insufficient knowledge of security best practices reduces the probability of users sticking to security policies and taking secure actions. Strategic technological investments and a deepened understanding of security measures synergistically enhance defensive capabilities
5	[68]	Insider threats	The healthcare sector encounters a substantial cyber security threat from internal employees or different users with malicious intentions. It poses a substantial risk to the safety and trustworthiness of crucial data and applications. User awareness training and strict access control mechanisms can reduce the threat malicious insiders pose
6	[69]	Phishing	Phishing attacks aim to trick users into divulging their passwords or other critical personal information that malevolent individuals can exploit

(*continued*)

Table 3. (*continued*)

S. No	Ref. No	Attacks	Description
7	[70]	Legacy Systems	It is critical to replace ancient systems with a modern ecosystem. However, multiple healthcare organizations are careful about replacement and reluctant to shift from their current methods
8	[71]	Impact of cloud technology	Healthcare organizations are increasingly migrating to cloud computing to store and oversee petabytes of confidential data. A higher number of website users directly correlates with an increased probability of a cyber-attack

efforts to reduce the occurrence of a cyber-attack. The existing cyber security defensive approach for healthcare organizations is illustrated in Fig. 3. The primary objective is to determine and address any vulnerabilities, protection risks, and organization data. The potential risk-mitigation procedures contain: a) deploying intrusion detection systems and defensive techniques, b) continuously upgrading software and hardware, and c) training employees with optimal cyber security practices.

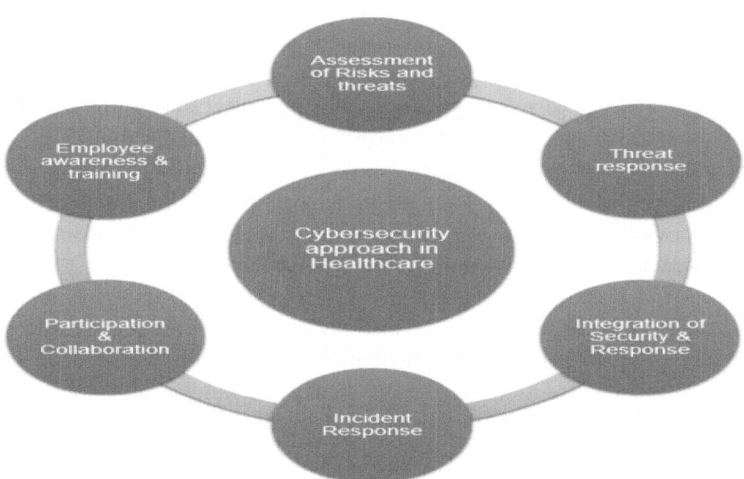

Fig. 3. Cyber security defenses for healthcare.

Healthcare organizations face unique cyber security challenges due to the sensitivity of patient information and the growing use of interconnected medical devices. Implementing effective mitigation techniques can help protect against cyber-attacks. Multi-factor authentication adds a layer of security beyond a standard login credentials, while encryption ensures that, even if attackers access data, they cannot interpret or use it without encryption keys [72]. Regular software updates help reduce vulnerabilities that cybercriminals may exploit in outdated systems. Phishing remains a common attack method in healthcare, and employee awareness training plays a crucial role in mitigating this risk [31]. Routine backups enable data restoration if data is lost or encrypted. A zero-trust model, where no one is trusted by default within or outside the network, requires continual verification of each access request [73]. Limiting the amount of sensitive data retained and regulating access further reduces the risk of breaches [74]. Finally, compliance with legislation ensures that healthcare organisations follow best practices in cyber security, safeguarding patient data [75].

5 Discussion

Inadequate security measures in the healthcare system can develop problems among patients and physicians about potential information violations. It distracts them from more important matters like providing medical care to the patients. Healthcare organizations should have an exhaustive control and response process to monitor and address document access. In e-health, it is crucial to eliminate all existing exposures and medical data breaches. Data protection may compromise the integrity of data. The transmission of sensitive data across several communication channels can make it vulnerable to a security violation. Transient compromise of data integrity can occur through a data communication link. Human error is an added risk that needs to be effectively addressed. The broadcast of inaccurate information and the inadequate handling of sensitive data expose healthcare organizations to the possibility of data loss. The security of information system security has become widely acknowledged as a crucial challenge in the realm of business.

The NIS1 and NIS2 directives represent significant advancements in enhancing cyber security within the EU healthcare sector. NIS2, in particular, addresses NIS1's limitations by expanding its scope, introducing more stringent measures, and standardizing legislation throughout the EU. It complements existing regulations such as GDPR by prioritizing network and systems security, ensuring healthcare infrastructure is resilient against cyber-attacks, and establishing more stringent governance and accountability frameworks within healthcare organizations. The attacks get increasingly refined with the ongoing growth of enhanced cyber security standards and technology. Using verified algorithms and products is important to minimize the possibilities of security breaches, software defects, and system failures. Cyber security methods should serve as a security filter rather than aggravating the issue by producing inconvenience and unreliability. Aligning cyber security and patient safety programs will encourage organizations to optimize clinical results by decreasing disturbances that could compromise patient information security and privacy, providing uninterrupted conditions of sufficient, high-quality care. The summary of advantages of applying robust cyber security in healthcare organizations are summarized in Fig. 4.

The next generation of cyber security revolves around adopting and innovating to establish a symbiotic interaction between humans and machines to fight against sophisticated attackers. Organizations can adopt this approach to enhance their probability of prevailing intricate, developed, and multi-vector attacks. The integration of AI into cyber

Fig. 4. Advantages of robust cyber security in healthcare organizations

security is pushed by its capability to assess extensive amounts of data and predict future possibilities. Healthcare organizations can enforce corrective actions once the damage has been imposed due to a system malfunction or cyber-attacks. Enforcing a proactive approach for obsolete systems is recommended to control future problems. The growing utilization of IT in healthcare has delivered edges such as improved information exchange, the automation of interconnected process activities, and enhanced interaction between clinical practitioners attending to the patients. The open challenges of cyber security in healthcare systems are demonstrated in Fig. 5.

A critical hypothesis for healthcare facilities to cover every network segment is crucial. It is likewise complex to forecast the possible threats that may arise. However, providing adequate security standards across the entire system is imperative. The exponential increase in cyber-attacks during the epidemic enabled the acquisition of essential facts about cyber security weaknesses associated with healthcare. In cyber security training, personnel can show greater vigilance in confirming the authenticity of any electronic communication. Furthermore, it can help implement more effective security measures and take the initiative to minimize the occurrence of human mistakes.

Healthcare cyber security research should prioritize technological advancements and address the evolving threat landscape. Tackling issues like legacy systems, human error, resource constraints, and data sharing requires interdisciplinary collaboration, continuous innovation, and rigorous security practices. Future research should aim to develop scalable, user-friendly, and cost-effective solutions to protect healthcare infrastructure and sensitive patient information [76]. AI and machine learning can enhance real-time breach detection, analyze patterns within large datasets, and mitigate risks automatically. Blockchain technology can provide decentralized, tamper-proof solutions for managing patient records, ensuring data integrity, and exploring privacy-preserving methods like differential privacy, federated learning, and homomorphic encryption. Emphasis should also be placed on the human aspects of cyber security, including countering social engineering, preventing phishing, and managing internal threats. Strengthening the cyber security of telemedicine platforms is essential to secure sensitive patient data and communications during remote consultations.

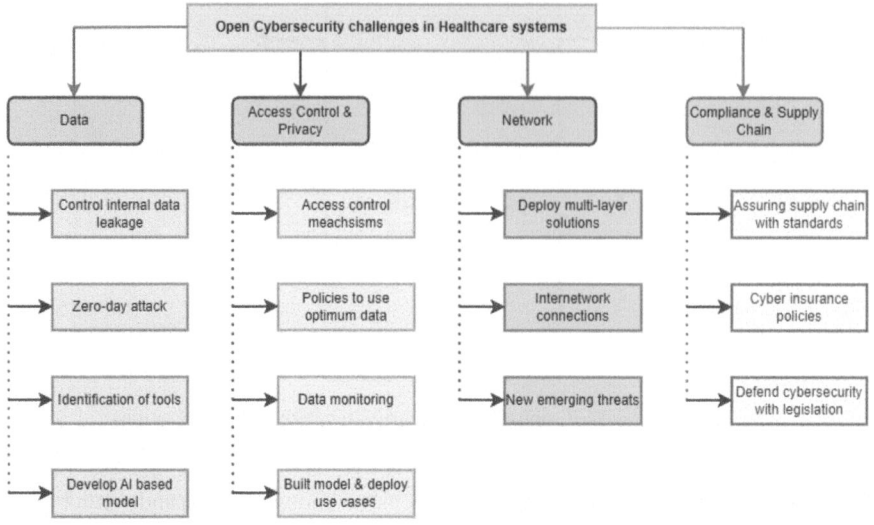

Fig. 5. Open cyber security challenges in healthcare systems

6 Conclusions

Healthcare organizations face significant cyber security vulnerabilities, highlighting the need for increased resource allocation to protect sensitive information. This study highlights the importance of cyber security applications and, using the PRISMA guidelines, reviews current tools and mitigation strategies employed in healthcare systems. Identified research gaps provide a foundation for future studies to expand existing knowledge in this area. Financial constraints challenge healthcare organizations in making cyber security investments. Balancing the immediate demands of patient care with the critical need for comprehensive cyber security requires strategic planning, sufficient funding, and a commitment to continuous improvement. Despite the availability of cyber security tools and mitigation techniques, healthcare organizations struggle to effectively implement and manage these solutions. Legacy systems, regulatory complexities, fragmented IT environments, and the evolving nature of cyber threats complicate efforts to achieve robust security. Overcoming these challenges demands an integrated approach, combining appropriate tools, staff training, regulatory expertise, and ongoing investments in emerging technologies like AI and automation.

References

1. Rejeb, A., et al.: Unleashing the power of internet of things and blockchain: a comprehensive analysis and future directions. Internet Things Cyber-Phys. Syst. **4**, 1–18 (2024). https://doi.org/10.1016/j.iotcps.2023.06.003
2. Javaid, M., Haleem, A., Singh, R.P., Suman, R.: Towards insighting cybersecurity for healthcare domains: A comprehensive review of recent practices and trends. Cyber Secur. Appl. **1**, 100016 (2023). https://doi.org/10.1016/j.csa.2023.100016

3. Hammi, B., Zeadally, S., Nebhen, J.: Security threats, countermeasures, and challenges of digital supply chains. ACM Comput. Surv. **55**, 1–40 (2023). https://doi.org/10.1145/3588999
4. Pool, J., Akhlaghpour, S., Fatehi, F., Burton-Jones, A.: A systematic analysis of failures in protecting personal health data: a scoping review. Int. J. Inf. Manage. **74**, 102719 (2024). https://doi.org/10.1016/j.ijinfomgt.2023.102719
5. Nemec Zlatolas, L., Welzer, T., Lhotska, L.: Data breaches in healthcare: security mechanisms for attack mitigation. Cluster Comput. (2024). https://doi.org/10.1007/s10586-024-04507-2
6. Barik, K., Misra, S., Konar, K., Fernandez-Sanz, L., Koyuncu, M.: Cybersecurity deep: approaches, attacks dataset, and comparative study. Appl. Artif. Intell. **36**, 2055399 (2022). https://doi.org/10.1080/08839514.2022.2055399
7. Barik, K., Misra, S.: Adversarial attack defense analysis: an empirical approach in cybersecurity perspective. Softw. Impacts. **21**, 100681 (2024). https://doi.org/10.1016/j.simpa.2024.100681
8. Salama, R., Altrjman, C., Al-Turjman, F.: Healthcare cybersecurity challenges: a look at current and future trends. In: Computational Intelligence and Blockchain in Complex Systems, pp. 97–111. Elsevier (2024). https://doi.org/10.1016/B978-0-443-13268-1.00003-0
9. Barik, K., Misra, S.: IDS-Anta: An open-source code with a defense mechanism to detect adversarial attacks for intrusion detection system. Softw. Impacts. **21**, 100664 (2024). https://doi.org/10.1016/j.simpa.2024.100664
10. Tonetto, L.M., et al.: Information and communication technologies in emergency care services for patients with COVID-19: a multi-national study. Int. J. Prod. Res. **61**, 8384–8400 (2023). https://doi.org/10.1080/00207543.2021.1967501
11. Cartwright, A.J.: The elephant in the room: cybersecurity in healthcare. J. Clin. Monit. Comput. **37**, 1123–1132 (2023). https://doi.org/10.1007/s10877-023-01013-5
12. Aslan, Ö., Aktuğ, S.S., Ozkan-Okay, M., Yilmaz, A.A., Akin, E.: A comprehensive review of cyber security vulnerabilities, threats, attacks, and solutions. Electronics **12**, 1333 (2023). https://doi.org/10.3390/electronics12061333
13. Firat Kilincer, I., Ertam, F., Sengur, A., Tan, R.-S., Rajendra Acharya, U.: Automated detection of cybersecurity attacks in healthcare systems with recursive feature elimination and multilayer perceptron optimization. Biocybern. Biomed. Eng. **43**, 30–41 (2023). https://doi.org/10.1016/j.bbe.2022.11.005
14. Babu, E.S., Yadav, B.V.R.N., Nikhath, A.K., Nayak, S.R., Alnumay, W.: MediBlocks: secure exchanging of electronic health records (EHRs) using trust-based blockchain network with privacy concerns. Cluster Comput. **26**, 2217–2244 (2023). https://doi.org/10.1007/s10586-022-03652-w
15. Pimenta Rodrigues, G.A., et al.: Understanding data breach from a global perspective: incident visualization and data protection law review. Data. **9**, 27 (2024). https://doi.org/10.3390/data9020027
16. Almalawi, A., Khan, A.I., Alsolami, F., Abushark, Y.B., Alfakeeh, A.S.: Managing security of healthcare data for a modern healthcare system. Sensors. **23**, 3612 (2023). https://doi.org/10.3390/s23073612
17. Barik, K., Misra, S., Chockalingam, S., Hoffmann, M.: Data analytics, digital transformation, and cybersecurity perspectives in healthcare. In: Abie, H., Gkioulos, V., Katsikas, S., and Pirbhulal, S. (eds.) Secure and Resilient Digital Transformation of Healthcare. pp. 71–89. Springer Nature Switzerland, Cham (2024). https://doi.org/10.1007/978-3-031-55829-0_5
18. Clarke, M., Martin, K.: Managing cybersecurity risk in healthcare settings. Healthc. Manage. Forum **37**, 17–20 (2024). https://doi.org/10.1177/08404704231195804
19. Goenka, R., Chawla, M., Tiwari, N.: A comprehensive survey of phishing: mediums, intended targets, attack and defence techniques and a novel taxonomy. Int. J. Inf. Secur. **23**, 819–848 (2024). https://doi.org/10.1007/s10207-023-00768-x

20. Shinde, R., Patil, S., Kotecha, K., Potdar, V., Selvachandran, G., Abraham, A.: Securing AI - based healthcare systems using blockchain technology: a state-of-the-art systematic literature review and future research directions. Trans Emerg. Tel Tech. **35**, e4884 (2024). https://doi.org/10.1002/ett.4884
21. Puttkammer, N., et al.: Data for public health action: Creating informatics-savvy health organizations to support integrated disease surveillance and response. In: Modernizing Global Health Security to Prevent, Detect, and Respond, pp. 329–356. Elsevier (2024). https://doi.org/10.1016/B978-0-323-90945-7.00005-1
22. Lu, W.: Application cost of intelligent intrusion detection in medical logistics management under public cloud environment. Comput. Electr. Eng. **112**, 109014 (2023). https://doi.org/10.1016/j.compeleceng.2023.109014
23. Tin, D., Hata, R., Granholm, F., Ciottone, R.G., Staynings, R., Ciottone, G.R.: Cyberthreats: a primer for healthcare professionals. Am. J. Emerg. Med. **68**, 179–185 (2023). https://doi.org/10.1016/j.ajem.2023.04.001
24. Ksibi, S., Jaidi, F., Bouhoula, A.: A Comprehensive study of security and cyber-security risk management within e-health systems: synthesis, analysis and a novel quantified approach. Mobile Netw Appl. **28**, 107–127 (2023). https://doi.org/10.1007/s11036-022-02042-1
25. Bhuyan, S.S., et al.: Transforming healthcare cybersecurity from reactive to proactive: current status and future recommendations. J. Med. Syst. **44**, 98 (2020). https://doi.org/10.1007/s10916-019-1507-y
26. Bracciale, L., Loreti, P., Bianchi, G.: Cybersecurity vulnerability analysis of medical devices purchased by national health services. Sci. Rep. **13**, 19509 (2023). https://doi.org/10.1038/s41598-023-45927-1
27. Mejía-Granda, C.M., Fernández-Alemán, J.L., Carrillo-de-Gea, J.M., García-Berná, J.A.: Security vulnerabilities in healthcare: an analysis of medical devices and software. Med. Biol. Eng. Comput. **62**, 257–273 (2024). https://doi.org/10.1007/s11517-023-02912-0
28. Walker-Roberts, S., Hammoudeh, M., Dehghantanha, A.: A systematic review of the availability and efficacy of countermeasures to internal threats in healthcare critical infrastructure. IEEE Access. **6**, 25167–25177 (2018). https://doi.org/10.1109/ACCESS.2018.2817560
29. Szczepaniuk, H., Szczepaniuk, E.K.: Cryptographic evidence-based cybersecurity for smart healthcare systems. Inf. Sci. **649**, 119633 (2023). https://doi.org/10.1016/j.ins.2023.119633
30. Silvestri, S., Islam, S., Amelin, D., Weiler, G., Papastergiou, S., Ciampi, M.: Cyber threat assessment and management for securing healthcare ecosystems using natural language processing. Int. J. Inf. Secur. **23**, 31–50 (2024). https://doi.org/10.1007/s10207-023-00769-w
31. Barik, K., Konar, K., Banerjee, A., Das, S., Abirami, A.: An Exploration of Attack Patterns and Protection Approaches Using Penetration Testing. In: Hemanth, D.J., Pelusi, D., and Vuppalapati, C. (eds.) Intelligent Data Communication Technologies and Internet of Things,d pp. 491–503. Springer Nature Singapore, Singapore (2022). https://doi.org/10.1007/978-981-16-7610-9_36
32. Alrowais, F., Mohamed, H.G., Al-Wesabi, F.N., Al Duhayyim, M., Hilal, A.M., Motwakel, A.: Cyber attack detection in healthcare data using cyber-physical system with optimized algorithm. Comput. Electr. Eng. **108**, 108636 (2023). https://doi.org/10.1016/j.compeleceng.2023.108636
33. Khan, I.A., et al.: Fed-Inforce-Fusion: a federated reinforcement-based fusion model for security and privacy protection of IoMT networks against cyber-attacks. Inform. Fusion. **101**, 102002 (2024). https://doi.org/10.1016/j.inffus.2023.102002
34. Al-Hawawreh, M., Moustafa, N., Slay, J.: A threat intelligence framework for protecting smart satellite-based healthcare networks. Neural Comput. Applic. **36**, 15–35 (2024). https://doi.org/10.1007/s00521-021-06441-5

35. Nadhan, A.S., Jeena Jacob, I.: Enhancing healthcare security in the digital era: safeguarding medical images with lightweight cryptographic techniques in IoT healthcare applications. Biomed. Signal Process. Control **88**, 105511 (2024). https://doi.org/10.1016/j.bspc.2023.105511
36. Jerry-Egemba, N.: Safe and sound: Strengthening cybersecurity in healthcare through robust staff educational programs. Healthc. Manage. Forum **37**, 21–25 (2024). https://doi.org/10.1177/08404704231194577
37. Katagiri, N.: Defending medical facilities from cyber attacks: critical issues with the principle of due diligence in international law. In: International Review of Law, Computers & Technology,pp, pp. 1–20 (2023). https://doi.org/10.1080/13600869.2023.2183449
38. Demertzi, V., Demertzis, S., Demertzis, K.: An Overview of cyber threats, attacks and countermeasures on the primary domains of smart cities. Appl. Sci. **13**, 790 (2023). https://doi.org/10.3390/app13020790
39. Hossain, N.U.I., Rahman, S., Liza, S.A.: Cyber-susiliency index: a comprehensive resiliency-sustainability-cybersecurity index for healthcare supply chain networks. Decision Anal. J. **9**, 100319 (2023). https://doi.org/10.1016/j.dajour.2023.100319
40. J, A., Isravel, D.P., Sagayam, K.M., Bhushan, B., Sei, Y., Eunice, J.: Blockchain for healthcare systems: Architecture, security challenges, trends and future directions. J. Netw. Comput. Appl. **215**, 103633 (2023). https://doi.org/10.1016/j.jnca.2023.103633
41. Jaime, F.J., Muñoz, A., Rodríguez-Gómez, F., Jerez-Calero, A.: Strengthening privacy and data security in biomedical microelectromechanical systems by IoT communication security and protection in smart healthcare. Sensors. **23**, 8944 (2023). https://doi.org/10.3390/s23218944
42. Sutradhar, S., Karforma, S., Bose, R., Roy, S.: A Dynamic step-wise tiny encryption algorithm with fruit fly optimization for quality of service improvement in healthcare. Healthcare Analytics. **3**, 100177 (2023). https://doi.org/10.1016/j.health.2023.100177
43. Al-Hawawreh, M., Hossain, M.S.: A privacy-aware framework for detecting cyber attacks on internet of medical things systems using data fusion and quantum deep learning. Inform. Fusion. **99**, 101889 (2023). https://doi.org/10.1016/j.inffus.2023.101889
44. Omolara, A.E., et al.: The internet of things security: A survey encompassing unexplored areas and new insights. Comput. Secur. **112**, 102494 (2022). https://doi.org/10.1016/j.cose.2021.102494
45. Maurya, C., Chaurasiya, V.K.: Collusion-resistant and privacy-preserving data sharing scheme on outsourced data in e-healthcare system. Multimed Tools Appl. **82**, 40443–40472 (2023). https://doi.org/10.1007/s11042-023-15006-8
46. Nwafor, O., Ma, X., Johnson, N.A., Singh, R., Aron, R.: Differential impacts of technology-network structures on cost efficiency: knowledge spillovers in healthcare. J. Manag. Inf. Syst. **40**, 840–882 (2023). https://doi.org/10.1080/07421222.2023.2229126
47. Riggs, H., et al.: Impact, Vulnerabilities, and mitigation strategies for cyber-secure critical infrastructure. Sensors. **23**, 4060 (2023). https://doi.org/10.3390/s23084060
48. Gioulekas, F., et al.: A cybersecurity culture survey targeting healthcare critical infrastructures. Healthcare. **10**, 327 (2022). https://doi.org/10.3390/healthcare10020327
49. Barik, K., Misra, S., Sanz, L.F., Chockalingam, S.: Enhancing image data security using the APFB model. Connect. Sci. **36**, 2379275 (2024). https://doi.org/10.1080/09540091.2024.2379275
50. Gupta, B.B., Gaurav, A., Kumar Panigrahi, P.: Analysis of security and privacy issues of information management of big data in B2B based healthcare systems. J. Bus. Res. **162**, 113859 (2023). https://doi.org/10.1016/j.jbusres.2023.113859
51. Parker, M.: Managing threats to health data and information: toward security. In: Health Information Exchange, pp. 149–196. Elsevier (2023). https://doi.org/10.1016/B978-0-323-90802-3.00016-2

52. Al-Jaroodi, J., Mohamed, N., Abukhousa, E.: Health 4.0: On the way to realizing the healthcare of the future. IEEE Access **8**, 211189–211210 (2020). https://doi.org/10.1109/ACCESS.2020.3038858
53. Putra, K.T., Arrayyan, A.Z., Hayati, N., Firdaus, Damarjati, C., Bakar, A., Chen, H.-C.: A review on the application of internet of medical things in wearable personal health monitoring: a cloud-edge artificial intelligence approach. IEEE Access **12**, 21437–21452 (2024). https://doi.org/10.1109/ACCESS.2024.3358827
54. Almotairi, K.H.: Application of internet of things in healthcare domain. J. Umm Al-Qura Univ. Eng. Archit. **14**, 1–12 (2023). https://doi.org/10.1007/s43995-022-00008-8
55. Raghupathi, W., Raghupathi, V., Saharia, A.: Analyzing health data breaches: a visual analytics approach. AppliedMath. **3**, 175–199 (2023). https://doi.org/10.3390/appliedmath3010011
56. Messinis, S., Temenos, N., Protonotarios, N.E., Rallis, I., Kalogeras, D., Doulamis, N.: Enhancing internet of medical things security with artificial intelligence: a comprehensive review. Comput. Biol. Med. **170**, 108036 (2024). https://doi.org/10.1016/j.compbiomed.2024.108036
57. Ejiofor, O., Akinsola, A.: Securing The Future Of Healthcare: Building A Resilient Defense System For Patient Data Protection. (2024). https://doi.org/10.48550/ARXIV.2407.16170
58. Cazares, M., Fuertes, W., Andrade, R., Ortiz-Garcés, I., Rubio, M.S.: Protective factors for developing cognitive skills against cyberattacks. Electronics **12**, 4007 (2023). https://doi.org/10.3390/electronics12194007
59. Admass, W.S., Munaye, Y.Y., Diro, A.A.: Cyber security: state of the art, challenges and future directions. Cyber Secur. Appl. **2**, 100031 (2024)
60. Mehmood, A., Shafique, A., Alawida, M., Khan, A.N.: Advances and vulnerabilities in modern cryptographic techniques: a comprehensive survey on cybersecurity in the domain of machine/deep learning and quantum techniques. IEEE Access. **12**, 27530–27555 (2024)
61. Wenhua, Z., Qamar, F., Abdali, T.-A.N., Hassan, R., Jafri, S.T.A., Nguyen, Q.N.: Blockchain technology: security issues, healthcare applications. Chall. Future Trends. Electron. **12**, 546 (2023). https://doi.org/10.3390/electronics12030546
62. Barik, K., Misra, S., Fernandez-Sanz, L.: Adversarial attack detection framework based on optimized weighted conditional stepwise adversarial network. Int. J. Inf. Secur. **23**, 2353–2376 (2024). https://doi.org/10.1007/s10207-024-00844-w
63. Shandler, R., Gomez, M.A.: The hidden threat of cyber-attacks – undermining public confidence in government. J. Inform. Tech. Polit. **20**, 359–374 (2023). https://doi.org/10.1080/19331681.2022.2112796
64. Zhou, Z., Gaurav, A., Gupta, B.B., Hamdi, H., Nedjah, N.: A statistical approach to secure health care services from DDoS attacks during COVID-19 pandemic. Neural Comput. & Applic. **36**, 1–14 (2024). https://doi.org/10.1007/s00521-021-06389-6
65. Al-Hawawreh, M., Alazab, M., Ferrag, M.A., Hossain, M.S.: Securing the Industrial Internet of Things against ransomware attacks: a comprehensive analysis of the emerging threat landscape and detection mechanisms. J. Netw. Comput. Appl. **223**, 103809 (2024). https://doi.org/10.1016/j.jnca.2023.103809
66. Choi, S.J., Chen, M., Tan, X.: Assessing the impact of health information exchange on hospital data breach risk. Int. J. Med. Informatics **177**, 105149 (2023). https://doi.org/10.1016/j.ijmedinf.2023.105149
67. Riahi, E., Islam, M.S.: Employees' information security awareness (ISA) in public organisations: insights from cross-cultural studies in Sweden, France, and Tunisia. Behav. Inform. Technol. 1–23 (2024). https://doi.org/10.1080/0144929X.2024.2311734

68. Velagala, L.P., Hossain, G.: Analyzing insider threats and human factors in healthcare 5.0. In: 2023 IEEE 20th International Conference on Smart Communities: Improving Quality of Life using AI, Robotics and IoT (HONET), pp. 95–100. IEEE, Boca Raton, FL, USA (2023). https://doi.org/10.1109/HONET59747.2023.10374733
69. Daengsi, T., Pornpongtechavanich, P., Wuttidittachotti, P.: Cybersecurity awareness enhancement: a study of the effects of age and gender of thai employees associated with phishing attacks. Educ. Inf. Technol. **27**, 4729–4752 (2022). https://doi.org/10.1007/s10639-021-10806-7
70. Irani, Z., Abril, R.M., Weerakkody, V., Omar, A., Sivarajah, U.: The impact of legacy systems on digital transformation in European public administration: lesson learned from a multi case analysis. Gov. Inf. Q. **40**, 101784 (2023). https://doi.org/10.1016/j.giq.2022.101784
71. Hernandez-Jaimes, M.L., Martinez-Cruz, A., Ramírez-Gutiérrez, K.A., Feregrino-Uribe, C.: Artificial intelligence for IoMT security: a review of intrusion detection systems, attacks, datasets and Cloud–Fog–Edge architectures. Internet Things **23**, 100887 (2023). https://doi.org/10.1016/j.iot.2023.100887
72. Guo, P., Gong, C., Lin, X., Yang, Z., Zhang, Q.: Exploring the Adversarial Frontier: Quantifying Robustness via Adversarial Hypervolume. arXiv preprint arXiv:2403.05100. (2024)
73. Zhu, H., Xue, X., Xu, M., Kim, B.-G., Lyu, X., Rani, S.: Zero-trust blockchain-enabled secure next-generation healthcare communication network. IEEE Trans. Netw. Serv. Manage. (2024)
74. Barik, K., Misra, S., Mohan, R., Mishra, B.: AIoT and its trust models to enhance societal applications using intelligent technologies. In: Artificial Intelligence of Things for Achieving Sustainable Development Goals, pp. 311–334. Springer (2024)
75. Ibrahim, A.M., et al.: Balancing confidentiality and care coordination: challenges in patient privacy. BMC Nurs. **23**, 564 (2024)
76. Burke, W., Stranieri, A., Oseni, T., Gondal, I.: The need for cybersecurity self-evaluation in healthcare. BMC Med. Inform. Decis. Mak.Mak. **24**, 133 (2024)

Invited Paper from Keynotes

AI for Healthcare Security: The Intersection of Innovation and Resilience

Ankur Shukla[✉]

Department of Risk and Security (SEC-R), Institute for Energy Technology (IFE), Halden, Norway
ankur.shukla@ife.no

Abstract. The healthcare system is a primary target for cyber attackers due to its critical role in society and the sensitivity of the data it handles, such as personal health information (PHI). In recent years, artificial intelligence (AI) has driven significant advancements in efficiency, accuracy, and accessibility across healthcare. This paper explores the transformative role of AI in enhancing healthcare cybersecurity by improving resilience, automating incident response, and driving innovation in safeguarding sensitive medical data and systems. AI-powered solutions, including predictive analytics and anomaly detection, are revolutionizing traditional security practices, enabling healthcare organizations to anticipate and mitigate threats more effectively. Additionally, the paper provides an overview of various standards, guidelines, and legal frameworks that offer a structured approach to protecting sensitive healthcare information, ensuring compliance, and mitigating risks. This work is part of the invited talk presented at the SUNRISE (Secure and Resilient Digital Transformation of Healthcare) workshop in Bergen, Norway.

Keywords: Healthcare security · Artificial intelligence · Resilience

1 Introduction

The advancement of technology has led to innovations like electronic health records (EHR), wearable devices, telemedicine, digital twins, robotics, and 5G/6G networks that have improved remote care, enabled real-time data analysis, created personalized treatments, and made healthcare delivery more efficient [31,36,48,49]. The growing interconnectedness of these technologies enhances efficiency, automation, and remote monitoring for acute and chronic care, allowing healthcare professionals to adjust implants and other devices without invasive procedures. However, significant cybersecurity risks are associated with this interconnected digital infrastructure. The healthcare sector is among the most targeted sectors for cyberattacks, with threats ranging from ransomware to data breaches. There is a significant risk of affecting the safety, trust, and operations of the organization due to these attacks. In the digital healthcare landscape, privacy is also one of the most significant concerns, as people are increasingly exposed to risks such as unauthorized access, and data breaches involving sensitive health information [15].

AI enhances the efficiency of healthcare systems through technologies that are capable of reasoning and decision-making. It is being used to uncover patterns in complex data, such as identifying connections within genetic codes, improving diagnostics, personalizing treatment plans, and even helping in surgical procedures with advanced robotics. These innovations enable more accurate, efficient, and proactive healthcare solutions, ultimately improving patient outcomes and streamlining medical processes [56]. AI in the healthcare sector improves the efficiency of operations and plays a crucial role in managing risks and building resilience [73]. Building resilience in healthcare through AI involves the improvement of the system's ability to anticipate, adapt, and respond to challenges [17,50]. With its ability to detect patterns, predict risks, and automate responses, AI is transforming healthcare security. AI bridges the gap between innovation and resilience, ensuring secure and efficient healthcare delivery. As healthcare systems increasingly adopt digital technologies, robust security measures are paramount. Integrating AI into healthcare security represents a pivotal advancement at the intersection of innovation and resilience. AI offers transformative capabilities in enhancing the security of electronic health systems by providing continuous monitoring, advanced pattern recognition, and real-time threat response, which are crucial for protecting sensitive health data. The synergy of AI with other technologies, such as blockchain, further fortifies the security of electronic health records (EHRs), addressing challenges like interoperability and data security concerns [5,71].

In the past, many papers have discussed the different aspects of the application of AI in healthcare. Olawale et al. [46] presented a review that explores AI's transformative role in achieving sustainable goals, such as fostering resilient infrastructure, promoting inclusivity, and driving innovation. Kokate et al. [35] highlighted the need for robust healthcare security frameworks by analyzing trends, current vulnerabilities, and emerging technologies like blockchain, AI, and IoT. Al-Khateeb [3] discussed the transformative impact of AI, ML, and Big Data across healthcare sector, financial services, and energy. Vishwakarma et al. [67] analyses the role of artificial intelligence in developing a healthcare system that is resilient and sustainable, especially with the challenges witnessed during the COVID - 19 pandemic. Yeng et al. [72] presented a review to identify suitable AI methods and data sources for addressing the security challenges, focusing on enhancing healthcare staff's security practices and mitigating data breaches. Wen et al. [69] discussed the use of AI for security assurance in various application domains.

This paper explores the challenges, risks, and opportunities associated with using AI in healthcare security, emphasizing how AI enhances resilience by transforming cybersecurity practices through solutions like predictive analytics and automated incident response. It also examines ethical considerations, including concerns around data privacy, bias, and accountability, which are critical to the responsible implementation of AI in healthcare. Additionally, the transformative role of AI in driving innovation and strengthening cybersecurity is highlighted. The paper briefly reviews established standards, guidelines, and legal frameworks relevant to healthcare security, ensuring compliance, protecting sensitive healthcare information, and mitigating cybersecurity risks. Finally, it offers insights into future trends and emerging research directions in AI-driven healthcare cybersecurity.

The remainder of this paper is structured in the following manner: Sect. 2 discusses the challenges in healthcare security. Section 3 examines the role of AI for cybersecurity in healthcare, considering its application to enhance resilience and mitigate risks effectively. Section 4 explores how AI is building resilience in healthcare, focusing on AI-driven solutions such as predictive analytics, and automated incident response. Section 5 addresses the challenges and ethical considerations of AI, including concerns related to data privacy, bias, and accountability. Section 6 provides an overview of relevant guidelines, standards, regulations, and frameworks that ensure compliance and protect sensitive healthcare information. Section 7 outlines future trends and research directions in AI-driven healthcare cybersecurity. Section 8 concludes the paper.

2 Cybersecurity Challenges in the Healthcare

The cybersecurity of healthcare is a challenging and complex issue. It involves several difficulties and requires advanced strategies and innovative solutions. Some of these challenges include:

2.1 Data Privacy and Security

The healthcare system stores and processes sensitive patient information, including personal identification information (PII), PHI, medical history, diagnostic results, treatment plans, and financial records. Due to its sensitive nature, this data is a prime target for unauthorized access, breaches, and cyberattacks. Attackers may use AI-based automated tools to improve their ability to identify and exploit vulnerabilities [21]. Therefore, data privacy and security are the highest priority for organizations and security professionals [55].

2.2 Cybersecurity Threats

The integration of emerging technologies including IoT devices, cloud computing, AI, EHRs, and telemedicine platforms, brings several advantages and innovations to healthcare. While these innovations transform the potential of healthcare and improve patient care and efficiency of the operation, they also comes with cybersecurity threats and expand the attack surface for cybercriminals. Therefore, it is essential to address these challenges and develop robust security assurance frameworks to establish secure and interoperable technology ecosystems in healthcare [25,57,59].

2.3 Legal and Ethical Compliance

It is imperative that healthcare practices comply with regulations such as HIPAA in the United States (US) and GDPR in the European Union (EU). Failure to comply with these regulations can lead to serious financial penalties, legal consequences, damage to reputation, and interruptions in operations. Compliance with these regulations requires the implementation of different security measures, including robust protections for sensitive patient information, including privacy, cybersecurity, and data breach notification requirements.

Therefore, organizations must tackle these challenges, such as compliance with the global regulatory requirements, seamless technological integration, and heightened accountability while addressing ethical concerns related to patient privacy and trust [14,24].

2.4 Complexity of the System and Evolving Threats

The healthcare sectors have experienced evolving threats in the past few years that have amplified the existing challenges. These cyberattacks include ransomware, phishing, and advanced persistent threats (APTs). Threat actors try to exploit the existing vulnerabilities in healthcare systems to gain unauthorized access. The supply chain is also exploited by attackers to compromise sensitive information and gain access to healthcare networks [2].

Healthcare involves highly complex systems that include emerging technologies, interconnected networks, and third-party applications. The complexity of these systems makes it difficult to protect them from the various threats posed by cyberattacks, including data breaches, ransomware, unauthorized access, and malware. On the other hand, some healthcare organizations still depend on outdated legacy systems that need to be designed to counter modern cybersecurity threats. Attacks on these systems can exploit vulnerabilities, such as lack of encryption, unsupported software, or weak access controls, making them prime targets for cybercriminals. Sometimes, it is not cost-effective to replace these legacy systems due to the significant financial and operational challenges involved. Therefore, it is important to protect these systems from cybersecurity threats [64].

3 AI for Cybersecurity in Healthcare

This section explores the benefits of AI for enhancing cybersecurity in healthcare organizations (Fig. 1).

3.1 Threat Detection and Analysis

AI is important in enhancing the capability and efficiency of cybersecurity threat detection and analysis. The integration of AI, specifically machine learning and deep learning techniques, with the healthcare systems enhances the ability to

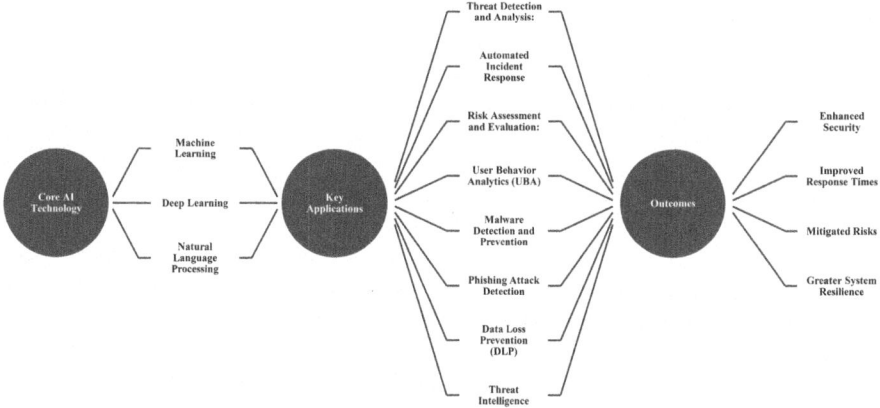

Fig. 1. AI for Cybersecurity in Healthcare.

identify, analyze, and provide the countermeasure of advanced cybersecurity threats, including network breaches, adversarial attacks, zero-day vulnerabilities, ransomware, phishing attacks, insider threats, and malware [6,60].

3.2 Automated Incident Response

The AI will benefit the development of automated incident response systems in the healthcare sector. Incidence response systems can detect, assess, and respond to security incidents promptly and proactively by applying ad AI algorithms, machine learning methods, and real-time threat intelligence data. AI-driven systems can identify security breaches, reduce response time, and minimize the impact on organizations' networks and operational areas due to automated decision-making and orchestration [40,52].

3.3 Risk Assessment and Evaluation

AI can be helpful to improve the effectiveness and efficiency of the risk assessment and evaluation process. AI can be used to automate various risk management process, reducing the required efforts and resources while minimizing human error by ensuring greater accuracy and completeness throughout the process. AI tools are useful for identifying potential threats, managing identified risks proactively, and automating real-time incident response. Additionally, AI can assist management in making informed decisions related to the risks by analyzing data, providing predictive insights, and recommending appropriate actions. AI can help to ensure a more flexible and responsive approach to risk management, enhancing overall organization resilience [34,42,68].

3.4 User Behavior Analytics (UBA)

In cybersecurity, UBA monitors user behavior on a network using data analytics, AI, and machine learning to model standard patterns of behavior and identify deviations that could signal potential security threats[1]. Analyzing patterns in user activity, AI can pinpoint unusual behaviors that may indicate an insider threat or unauthorized access to sensitive data. UBA helps healthcare organizations detect and mitigate insider threats, which can be a leading source of data breaches [23,45].

3.5 Malware Detection and Prevention

The rise in malware presents a significant threat to security and safety within the healthcare sector. AI-driven malware detection and prevention tools can be very useful for detecting and preventing malicious software from compromising the healthcare networks. Unlike traditional signature-based detection methods that struggle with new or evolving malware, AI based systems analyze behavior and characteristics to identify threats, even those previously unseen [19,22].

3.6 Phishing Attack Detection

Phishing attack is one of the most common threats to healthcare systems. AI plays a crucial role in reducing this risk by improving the detection of phishing and email scams. It analyzes the email content, sender behavior, and metadata to identify the potential phishing attempts. As a result, the success rate of these scams is significantly decreased, protecting both employees and patients from data theft and fraud in the healthcare sector [9].

3.7 Data Loss Prevention (DLP)

AI-driven DLP technology significantly prevents unauthorized access to or leakage of confidential healthcare information. This technology can monitor data usage and detect unusual behavior related to data transfers or access to sensitive patient records. AI-driven DLP technology is crucial to preventing unauthorized access to sensitive healthcare data. It monitors data usage and detects unusual behavior related to data transfers or patient records access. In the case of a potential breach, the AI system can block the action and notify the security teams, helping to protect patient information and maintain compliance with data protection regulations [30].

3.8 Threat Intelligence

The use of AI can significantly enhance threat intelligence by identifying, analyzing, and mitigating potential cybersecurity risks in healthcare.AI can be integrated into threat intelligence systems to aggregate and analyze large amount of data from multiple sources to detect and prioritize threats more accurately. AI systems use this intelligence to provide relevant security measures [62].

---
[1] https://www.ibm.com/topics/user-behavior-analytics.

4 Building Resilience with AI in Healthcare

AI significantly contributes to building resilience in the healthcare sector through increased productivity, improved patient outcomes, and support for healthcare professionals [43]. AI is helping to build resilience in healthcare in several ways, some of which are discussed below:

4.1 Predictive Analytics for Proactive Decision-Making

AI is transforming healthcare through advancements in predictive analytics that improve patient outcomes and operational efficiency. By leveraging machine learning and large datasets, AI identifies trends and predicts potential risks, enhancing healthcare systems' resilience. This technology enables personalized treatment and better resource management. Additionally, AI enhances hospital efficiency by optimizing resource allocation and patient flow [4]. AI can also be effective in primary healthcare clinical decision support systems, including diagnosis support, treatment recommendations, and complication prediction that improves clinical management, patient safety, and reducing physician workload [29].

4.2 Supply Chain Optimization

The healthcare industry encounters a variety of challenges, including inefficiency and high supply chain costs. Adopting a more effective and sustainable approach to address these issues and adjusting to significant shifts in public health and the global economy is crucial. AI can play a key role by enabling intelligent, data-driven decisions that help identify the optimal supply chain model for healthcare. The use of this approach will lead to greater efficiency, a reduction in costs, and long-term sustainability [17, 38].

4.3 Risk Assessment and Mitigation

AI is emerging as an essential innovation in risk management in the healthcare sector that provides more accurate, efficient, and predictive capabilities than conventional methods. By employing advanced data analytics, AI can identify potential risks with greater precision, assess their impact, and recommend proactive and adaptive mitigation strategies [12]. From a cybersecurity perspective, Security vulnerabilities and misconfigurations in healthcare systems can pose significant risks and create major attack surfaces. AI-driven risk assessment methods can be beneficial in evaluating potential vulnerabilities, threats, and risks. This enables organizations to prioritize security efforts by calculating and predicting a risk score indicating key vulnerabilities and their potential consequences [47].

4.4 Enhancing Remote Care

AI-powered remote care integrates software and hardware solutions to ensure reliable, efficient, and secure systems. The systems monitor and forecast vital signs while also identifying and categorizing physical activities such as monitoring a person's heartbeat, blood pressure, and oxygen saturation. AI also detects patient activities such as falls and mobility issues. AI-based wearables and sensors provide continuous real-time data, enabling anomaly detection and personalized care by analyzing patterns and trends in patient data, improving disease risk assessment and early intervention [32,66]. AI can also enhance virtual medical consultations in healthcare, particularly for individuals managing chronic illnesses [18].

AI in healthcare must remain resilient throughout its entire lifecycle. AI systems should evolve and adapt in accordance with relevant standards, rules, and regulations. As discussed in Sect. 5, there are several key challenges associated with using AI in the healthcare sector. Therefore, AI should be designed with resilience in mind to address these challenges, which could threaten the safety and fundamental rights of millions of individuals [53].

5 Challenges and Ethical Considerations of AI

AI has revolutionized healthcare, from clinical applications like diagnostics to workflow optimization and symptom assessment via health apps. However, AI in healthcare comes with several challenges, including the technical, operational, ethical, and legal challenges that must be addressed during the different stages of the lifecycle [7,26]. Some of these challenges include (Fig. 2).

5.1 Technical Challenges

Data Quality and Availability: The effectiveness of AI relies on various factors, such as the quality of data, its accuracy, completeness, consistency, and how timely it is. A poor quality of data can result in inaccurate predictions and biased models. To ensure that data can be used for analysis and model training, data engineers must build robust data pipelines to ensure seamless data flow [16].

Integration and Scalability: The integration and scalability of AI into existing healthcare infrastructure can be very challenging. This process includes identifying the relevant application scenarios, fine-tuning AI models to the appropriate scenarios, and ensuring the seamless integration of AI with the existing system. Comprehensive strategic planning and careful consideration are essential for the responsible integration of AI-driven tools and the effective large-scale deployment of AI in healthcare [20].

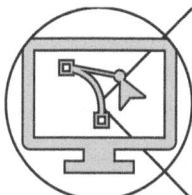
Technical Challenges
• Data Quality and Availability
• Integration and Scalability
• Regulatory Compliance
• Continuous Learning and Adaptation

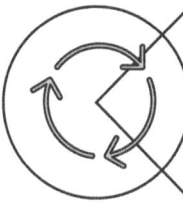
Operational Challenges
• Interoperability and Visualization
• Human-Machine Interaction
• Decision Support Systems and Data Sharing
• Interpretability vs. Performance Trade-off
• Cost
• Workforce Training
• Trust and Acceptance

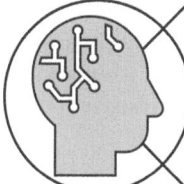
Ethical Challenges
• Privacy
• Bias
• Transparency
• Opacity and Accountability

Fig. 2. Challenges and Ethical Considerations of AI.

Regulatory Compliance: The integration of AI into healthcare poses several regulatory compliance challenges that must be addressed to ensure the secure, safe, and efficient application of AI. These challenges necessitate a comprehensive understanding of compliance frameworks. Due to the advancement of AI in healthcare, a number of tools and applications have been developed, many of which lack regulatory approvals, highlighting the urgent need for intense regulatory supervision [41].

Continuous Learning and Adaptation: AI systems in healthcare require continuous learning and adaptation to address the dynamic nature of medical data, which is essential for their long-term effectiveness, safety, and success in a rapidly evolving medical field [65]. On the other hand, the dynamic and ever-evolving nature of AI necessitates the continuing education program for healthcare providers to stay informed about the newest developments and optimal practices. [20].

5.2 Operational Challenges

There are several operational challenges of AI in healthcare, some of them are as follows [37,54]:

Interoperability and Visualization: The interoperability of AI with the existing healthcare infrastructure and effective visualization are significant operational challenges. The advanced methods are needed to enhance the understanding and verification of AI-generated explanations, particularly in critical healthcare applications [54].

Human-Machine Interaction: A key operational challenge in AI for healthcare is the lack of explanations that are tailored to different users and the absence of adequate feedback systems. This makes it difficult to integrate transparency, ethics, and good decision-making into AI systems [54].

Decision Support Systems and Data Sharing: One of the operational challenges of AI in healthcare is integrating unstructured medical data and ensuring effective collaboration among stakeholders. Moreover, data sharing is vulnerable to security and privacy breaches, so security and privacy during transfer require a robust and adaptive approach [54].

Interpretability vs. Performance Trade-Off: A key challenge of AI in healthcare is achieving the right balance between the complexity of the model and its transparency and interpretability. This requires using approaches that align with human reasoning while preserving the model's accuracy and effectiveness [54].

Cost: AI technology implementation and maintenance can be expensive especially in smaller healthcare organizations. Therefore, it is crucial to balance the cost with potential benefits [33].

Workforce Training: Healthcare professionals require the required skills development and training to effectively use AI tools specially for critical healthcare. It is also important to ensure the working staff are comfortable with the use of AI tools maximize its potential [58].

Trust and Acceptance: As AI technologies, including generative and ambient AI solutions, become more common in healthcare, the trust of healthcare professionals is vital for their successful adoption and effectiveness. Healthcare organizations need to establish methods for assessing the factors that influence trust and acceptance of AI in clinical workflows. This validation is crucial to improve the adoption and impact of AI systems, ensuring that both healthcare providers and patients have confidence in them [27,61].

5.3 Ethical Challenges

There are several ethical challenges to using AI in the healthcare sector; some of the challenges are as follows:

Privacy: Using AI in healthcare poses a number of ethical challenges, including ensuring that sensitive patient data is protected from unauthorized access. There are major concerns regarding the privacy violations of AI systems that handle sensitive data processes. [70]. Hence, AI systems need to be designed to protect the privacy and compliance with the data protection regulations.

Bias: The evolution and integration of AI in healthcare come with several challenges, including bias, discrimination, and unjustified actions. The present bias in AI algorithms raises ethical concerns requiring careful examination. Addressing these issues adequately is essential since biases in data or decision-making processes within algorithms could result in disparities in healthcare outcomes [28, 39].

Transparency: AI decision-making must be transparent and accountable to build trust and ensure explainability for patients and healthcare providers. Transparency makes algorithms understandable and provides stakeholders with detailed information on processes, datasets, training, validation, and model outcomes [10].

Opacity and Accountability: Opacity and accountability are significant ethical challenges in AI healthcare. Many AI systems function as "black boxes," complication the understanding of their decision-making processes, which reduces trust and clarity. It is more difficult to determine who is accountable for errors when it is unclear whether technologists, their systems, or clinicians are at fault. Overcoming these challenges requires improving AI transparency and creating clear accountability frameworks to ensure ethical and responsible decision-making in healthcare [60].

6 Guidelines, Standards, Regulations and Frameworks

In this section, some of the existing guidelines, standards, regulations, and frameworks applicable to AI and cybersecurity in the healthcare sector have been discussed.

6.1 Guidelines and Standards

NIST AI Risk Management Framework (AI RMF): NIST's AI Risk Management Framework[2] is a comprehensive guide that helps organizations manage

---

[2] https://www.nist.gov/itl/ai-risk-management-framework.

the risks associated with AI systems. The document emphasizes trustworthiness and offers guidelines for AI system design, development, use, and evaluation. The AI RMF consists of four core functions:

- Govern: In the govern function, processes, structures, and practices are established to align AI systems with organizational values, evaluate potential impacts, and manage risks throughout the AI system's lifecycle.
- Map: The map function aims to identify and understand AI risks in their context, scope, and nature.
- Measure: The measure functions analyze, assess, benchmark, and monitor AI risks and their impacts using quantitative, qualitative, and mixed methods tools, techniques, and methodologies.
- Manage: It involves consistently allocating resources to the risks that have been identified and assessed as defined by the governance function.

ISO/IEC 27001: The ISO 27001 standard covers information security management systems (ISMS). The system helps healthcare organizations manage risk in a systematic way that protects data and ensures compliance with regulations[3].

ISO/IEC 27701: This standard extends ISO/IEC 27001 and ISO/IEC 27002 for privacy information management system (PIMS). It is particularly relevant for all organizations, including PII controllers and processors, handling PII within an ISMS. In the context of healthcare organizations, it can be applied to PHI[4].

ISO/IEC 42001: The standard specifies how AI systems should be managed within organizations. It provides a structured framework that outlines a process for establishing, implementing, maintaining, and continuously improving Artificial Intelligence Management Systems (AIMS). This standard applies to any organization using AI, including healthcare, helping them manage risks and demonstrate reliable, transparent AI practices[5].

ISO/IEC 23894 : This standard provides guidance for managing AI-related risks in organizations that develop, deploy, or use AI systems, helping integrate risk management into AI activities and ensuring effective implementation of AI risk management processes[6].

OECD AI Principles: The OECD AI principles guide stakeholders in developing trustworthy AI and provide policymakers with recommendation for creating effective AI policies[7].

---

[3] https://www.iso.org/standard/27001.
[4] https://www.iso.org/standard/71670.html.
[5] https://www.iso.org/standard/81230.html.
[6] https://www.iso.org/standard/77304.html.
[7] https://www.oecd.org/en/topics/sub-issues/ai-principles.html.

6.2 Regulations

General Data Protection Regulation (GDPR): Regulations set guidelines for the collection and processing of personal information by the EU. Additionally, it has implications for AI systems handling healthcare data, as well as ensuring data security and privacy[8].

Health Insurance Portability and Accountability Act (HIPAA): The HIPAA defines the criteria for protecting sensitive patient information in the US. Any organization that handles PHI must ensure that all necessary physical, network, and procedural security protocols are implemented and adhered to[9].

European Cyber Resilience Act: The act specifies security requirements for digital hardware and software products in the EU. It requires manufacturers to prioritize security throughout the entire product lifecycle[10].

EU AI Act: The AI Act is an EU regulation aimed at promoting human-centric AI while safeguarding health, safety, and fundamental rights. It prohibits certain AI practices outright and imposes strict requirements on high-risk AI systems. It prohibits certain AI practices outright and imposes strict requirements on high-risk AI systems[11].

6.3 Frameworks

NIST Cybersecurity Framework (CSF): This framework is voluntary and includes standards, guidelines, and best practices to manage risks related to cybersecurity. It is commonly employed in the healthcare sector to improve the security and resilience of critical infrastructure[12].

HITRUST CSF: The HITRUST Common Security Framework (CSF) consolidates various standards and regulations to create a thorough method for managing information security, especially in the healthcare sector[13].

7 Future Trends and Research Directions

This section discusses the future trends and research directions of AI in healthcare resilience and cybersecurity. The following discusses some future trends and research directions. [1]:

---

[8] https://gdpr-info.eu/.
[9] https://www.hhs.gov/hipaa/index.html.
[10] https://digital-strategy.ec.europa.eu/en/policies/cyber-resilience-act.
[11] https://artificialintelligenceact.eu/.
[12] https://www.nist.gov/cyberframework.
[13] https://hitrustalliance.net/hitrust-framework.

7.1 Continuous Innovation in AI Applications

There will be ongoing innovation in AI technology that drives advancements in both healthcare and cybersecurity. The evolution of AI technologies will offer new solutions to address complex challenges, such as real-time threat detection in cybersecurity and personalized medicine in healthcare [1].

7.2 Human-AI Collaboration

The future work will focus more on human-AI collaboration, where AI systems and humans work together synergistically to augment rather than replace human capabilities. Humans contribute specialized expertise to complex decision-making, while AI offers data-driven insights. As AI progresses, the main focus will be on enhancing and refining human and AI interactions to ensure their effectiveness in assisting users in healthcare [44].

7.3 Quantum AI (QAI)

Quantum AI combines quantum computing with artificial intelligence to increase computation speed and power through the use of quantum principles like superposition and entanglement. This advancement enhances machine learning, data analysis, and optimization capabilities for practical applications in healthcare that enables faster and more accurate diagnoses and personalized treatment options. The future research works will be primarily focuses on leveraging quantum AI for processing medical data, predictive analytics, and optimizing healthcare outcomes [13,51]. Quantum AI is also very useful in enhance the cybersecurity in the healthcare sectors [8].

7.4 Neuro-Symbolic AI

Neuro-symbolic AI is a rapidly evolving field that combines the strengths of deep neural networks (subsymbolic) and symbolic knowledge graphs to improve explainability and safety in AI systems. Future work will focus more on this approach, which enables AI to reason, learn, and generalize in a way that is understandable to human experts. This approach addresses key challenges in fields like cybersecurity and privacy, where explainability and accuracy are crucial [13].

7.5 Developing Global Standards and Regulations

The development of comprehensive national, regional, and international guidelines will be emphasized to ensure AI contributes to equitable and fair healthcare systems worldwide. These guidelines must address critical challenges, including accuracy, transparency, security, informed consent, data privacy, and ethical considerations in the use of health data. To foster trust in AI-driven healthcare solutions, it is crucial to establish clear standards and regulations that promote fairness and health equity [11].

7.6 AI and Blockchain

In the healthcare industry, blockchain and AI are transforming technologies. As a result, more emphasis will be placed on integrating these technologies to create robust AI models for e-Health, leveraging blockchain's open network for secure data sharing and authorization. Integrating these technologies can improve healthcare efficiency, reduce costs, and democratize access, enabling healthcare professionals to access secure patient records and deliver better outcomes [63].

8 Conclusion

Healthcare remains a prominent target for cyberattacks due to its critical role in society and the sensitive data it holds, such as protected health information. In this paper, we explore AI's transformative potential in enhancing healthcare cybersecurity and resilience. Using artificial intelligence, healthcare organizations can anticipate, detect, and mitigate threats more effectively by enabling predictive analytics, anomaly detection, and automated incident response.

As AI introduces opportunities for innovation and resilience, its implementation also brings challenges, particularly when it comes to addressing ethical issues such as data privacy, bias, and accountability. Compliance with standards, guidelines, and legal frameworks that offer structured approaches to risk mitigation and compliance is critical to the responsible deployment of AI in healthcare security.

The insights presented in this paper, including discussions on current practices, challenges, and future trends, emphasize the need for ongoing research and development in AI-driven cybersecurity solutions as healthcare systems continue their digital transformation; leveraging AI responsibly and effectively will be essential for building a secure, resilient, and innovative future for the healthcare.

References

1. Achuthan, K., Ramanathan, S., Srinivas, S., Raman, R.: Advancing cybersecurity and privacy with artificial intelligence: current trends and future research directions. Front. Big Data **7**, 1497535 (2024)
2. Admass, W.S., Munaye, Y.Y., Diro, A.A.: Cyber security: state of the art, challenges and future directions. Cyber Secur. Appl. **2**, 100031 (2024)
3. Al-Khateeb, B.: Intersection of artificial intelligence, machine learning, and big data in transforming healthcare management, financial services, and sustainable energy solutions. Emerg. Trends Mach. Intell. Big Data **15**(11), 12–19 (2023)
4. Ali, U., Russell, S.: Ai and the future of healthcare: Enhancing predictive analytics for better outcomes
5. Ara, A., Mifa, A.F.: Integrating artificial intelligence and big data in mobile health: a systematic review of innovations and challenges in healthcare systems. Global Mainstream J. Business, Econom., Develop. Project Manage. **3**(01), 01–16 (2024)
6. Arefin, S.: Strengthening healthcare data security with AI-powered threat detection. Int. J. Sci. Res. Manage. (IJSRM) **12**(10), 1477–1483 (2024)

7. Aung, Y.Y., Wong, D.C., Ting, D.S.: The promise of artificial intelligence: a review of the opportunities and challenges of artificial intelligence in healthcare. Br. Med. Bull. **139**(1), 4–15 (2021)
8. Azeez, M., et al.: Quantum AI for cybersecurity in financial supply chains: enhancing cryptography using random security generators. World J. Adv. Res. Rev. **23**(1), 2443–2451 (2024)
9. Bauskar, S.R., Madhavaram, C.R., Galla, E.P., Sunkara, J.R., Gollangi, H.K.: Ai-driven phishing email detection: leveraging big data analytics for enhanced cybersecurity. Libr. Prog. Int. **44**(3), 7211–7224 (2024)
10. Bernal, J., Mazo, C.: Transparency of artificial intelligence in healthcare: insights from professionals in computing and healthcare worldwide. Appl. Sci. **12**(20), 10228 (2022)
11. Bouderhem, R.: Shaping the future of AI in healthcare through ethics and governance. Human. Social Sci. Commun. **11**(1), 1–12 (2024)
12. Chaiwong, N., Srisai, A.: Risk management using AI: developing robust models for identifying and mitigating emerging financial risks. Asian Am. Res. Lett. J. **1**(7), 33–40 (2024)
13. Chauhan, D., Ranka, P., Bahad, P., Pathak, R.: Applications of quantum artificial intelligence: a systematic review. In: Integration of AI, Quantum Computing, and Semiconductor Technology, pp. 159–182 (2025)
14. Cochran, K.A.: Legal and compliance considerations in cybersecurity. In: Cochran, K.A. (ed.) Cybersecurity Essentials: Practical Tools for Today's Digital Defenders, pp. 431–463. Apress, Berkeley, CA (2024). https://doi.org/10.1007/979-8-8688-0432-8_15
15. Coventry, L., Branley, D.: Cybersecurity in healthcare: a narrative review of trends, threats and ways forward. Maturitas **113**, 48–52 (2018)
16. Deekshith, A.: Data engineering for AI: optimizing data quality and accessibility for machine learning models. Int. J. Manage. Educ. Sustain. Develop. **4**(4), 1–33 (2021)
17. Deveci, M.: Effective use of artificial intelligence in healthcare supply chain resilience using fuzzy decision-making model. Soft Comput. (2023). https://doi.org/10.1007/s00500-023-08906-2
18. Dhunnoo, P., McGuigan, K., O'Rourke, V., McCann, M.: Artificial intelligence enhancement for remote virtual consultations in healthcare provision for patients with chronic conditions. In: Stephanidis, C., Antona, M., Ntoa, S., Salvendy, G. (eds.) HCI International 2023 Posters: 25th International Conference on Human-Computer Interaction, HCII 2023, Copenhagen, Denmark, July 23–28, 2023, Proceedings, Part II, pp. 45–50. Springer Nature Switzerland, Cham (2023). https://doi.org/10.1007/978-3-031-35992-7_7
19. Edward, A.: Leveraging ai to strengthen cybersecurity and mitigate ransomware threats in healthcare (2020)
20. Esmaeilzadeh, P.: Challenges and strategies for wide-scale artificial intelligence (AI) deployment in healthcare practices: A perspective for healthcare organizations. Artif. Intell. Med. **151**, 102861 (2024)
21. Færøy, F.L., Yamin, M.M., Shukla, A., Katt, B.: Automatic verification and execution of cyber attack on Iot devices. Sensors **23**(2), 733 (2023)
22. Faruk, M.J.H., et al.: Malware detection and prevention using artificial intelligence techniques. In: 2021 IEEE International Conference on Big Data (big data), pp. 5369–5377. IEEE (2021)

23. G. Martín, A., Fernández-Isabel, A., Martín de Diego, I., Beltrán, M.: A survey for user behavior analysis based on machine learning techniques: current models and applications. Appl. Intell. **51**(8), 6029–6055 (2021). https://doi.org/10.1007/s10489-020-02160-x
24. Galvão, A.M., Vaz, C.B., Pinheiro, M., Pais, C.: Ethical and legal aspects of cybersecurity in health. ARIS-Adv. Res. Inform. Syst. Secur. **4**(1), 04–19 (2024)
25. Garcia-Perez, A., Cegarra-Navarro, J.G., Sallos, M.P., Martinez-Caro, E., Chinnaswamy, A.: Resilience in healthcare systems: cyber security and digital transformation. Technovation **121**, 102583 (2023)
26. Gerke, S., Minssen, T., Cohen, G.: Ethical and legal challenges of artificial intelligence-driven healthcare. In: Artificial Intelligence in Healthcare, pp. 295–336. Elsevier (2020)
27. Gille, F., Jobin, A., Ienca, M.: What we talk about when we talk about trust: theory of trust for AI in healthcare. Intell.-Based Med. **1**, 100001 (2020)
28. Giovanola, B., Tiribelli, S.: Beyond bias and discrimination: redefining the AI ethics principle of fairness in healthcare machine-learning algorithms. AI Society **38**(2), 549–563 (2023)
29. Gomez-Cabello, C.A., Borna, S., Pressman, S., Haider, S.A., Haider, C.R., Forte, A.J.: Artificial-intelligence-based clinical decision support systems in primary care: a scoping review of current clinical implementations. Europ. J. Investig. Health, Psychol. Educ. **14**(3), 685–698 (2024)
30. James, M.: Ai-powered identity governance and data loss prevention strategies in healthcare (2021)
31. Jørgensen, C.S., Shukla, A., Katt, B.: Digital twins in healthcare: security, privacy, trust and safety challenges. In: Katsikas, S., et al. (eds.) Computer Security. ESORICS 2023 International Workshops: CPS4CIP, ADIoT, SecAssure, WASP, TAURIN, PriST-AI, and SECAI, The Hague, The Netherlands, September 25–29, 2023, Revised Selected Papers, Part II, pp. 140–153. Springer Nature Switzerland, Cham (2024). https://doi.org/10.1007/978-3-031-54129-2_9
32. Kalusivalingam, A.K., Sharma, A., Patel, N., Singh, V.: Enhancing patient care through Iot-enabled remote monitoring and AI-driven virtual health assistants: Implementing machine learning algorithms and natural language processing. Int. J. AI ML **2**(3) (2021)
33. Kastrup, N., Holst-Kristensen, A.W., Valentin, J.B.: Landscape and challenges in economic evaluations of artificial intelligence in healthcare: a systematic review of methodology. BMC Digital Health **2**(1), 39 (2024)
34. Khatib, E., ZM, R., Al-Nakeeb, A.: The effect of AI on project and risk management in health care industry projects in the United Arab Emirates (UAE). Int. J. Appl. Eng. Res **6**(1) (2021)
35. Kokate, M.D., Gujar, S.N., Bangare, S.L., Dhabliya, D., Sharma, P., Patil, M.: Securing the future: Technological innovations for social medical public healthcare security. South Eastern European Journal of Public Health, pp. 12–23 (2024)
36. Kyrarini, M., Lygerakis, F., Rajavenkatanarayanan, A., Sevastopoulos, C., Nambiappan, H.R., Chaitanya, K.K., Babu, A.R., Mathew, J., Makedon, F.: A survey of robots in healthcare. Technologies **9**(1), 8 (2021)
37. Lee, D., Yoon, S.N.: Application of artificial intelligence-based technologies in the healthcare industry: opportunities and challenges. Int. J. Environ. Res. Public Health **18**(1), 271 (2021)
38. Long, P., Lu, L., Chen, Q., Chen, Y., Li, C., Luo, X.: Intelligent selection of healthcare supply chain mode-an applied research based on artificial intelligence. Front. Public Health **11**, 1310016 (2023)

39. LOUE, S.: Chapter thirteen. Bipolar Disorder in Later Life p. 234 (2007)
40. Maddireddy, B.R., Maddireddy, B.R.: Enhancing network security through AI-powered automated incident response systems. Int. J. Adv. Eng. Technol. Innov. **1**(02), 282–304 (2023)
41. Mennella, C., Maniscalco, U., De Pietro, G., Esposito, M.: Ethical and regulatory challenges of ai technologies in healthcare: A narrative review. Heliyon (2024)
42. Ning, Y., et al.: An ethics assessment tool for artificial intelligence implementation in healthcare: Care-AI. Nature Medicine, pp. 1–2 (2024)
43. Noorbakhsh-Sabet, N., Zand, R., Zhang, Y., Abedi, V.: Artificial intelligence transforms the future of health care. Am. J. Med. **132**(7), 795–801 (2019)
44. Ofusori, L., Bokaba, T., Mhlongo, S.: Artificial intelligence in cybersecurity: a comprehensive review and future direction. Appl. Artif. Intell. **38**(1), 2439609 (2024)
45. Olabanji, S.O., et al.: Ai-driven cloud security: Examining the impact of user behavior analysis on threat detection. Asian J. Res. Comput. Sci. **17**(3), 57–74 (2024)
46. Olawale, M.A., Ayeh, A.A., Adekola, F.O., Precious, A.S., Joshua, A.O., Timothy, O.: A review on the intersection of artificial intelligence on building resilient infrastructure, promoting inclusive and sustainable industrialization and fostering innovation. Int. J. Eng. Modern Technol **9**(3), 1–31 (2023)
47. Pattyam, S.P.: Artificial intelligence in cybersecurity: advanced methods for threat detection, risk assessment, and incident response. J.AI Healthcare Med. **1**(2), 83–108 (2021)
48. Pirbhulal, S., Abie, H., Shukla, A.: Towards a novel framework for reinforcing cybersecurity using digital twins in Iot-based healthcare applications. In: 2022 IEEE 95th Vehicular Technology Conference:(VTC2022-Spring), pp. 1–5. IEEE (2022)
49. Pirbhulal, S., Chockalingam, S., Shukla, A., Abie, H.: IoT cybersecurity in 5G and beyond: a systematic literature review. Int. J. Inform. Secur. **23**(4), 2827–2879 (2024). https://doi.org/10.1007/s10207-024-00865-5
50. Rane, N., Choudhary, S., Rane, J.: Artificial intelligence for enhancing resilience. J. Appl. Artif. Intell. **5**(2), 1–33 (2024)
51. Kala Rani, K.S., Priyadharsheni, J.M., Karthikeyan, B., Pugalendhi, G.S.: Chapter 14 Applications of quantum AI for healthcare. In: Raj, P., Kumar, A., Dubey, A.K., Bhatia, S., Manoj S, O. (eds.) Quantum Computing and Artificial Intelligence: Training Machine and Deep Learning Algorithms on Quantum Computers, pp. 271–288. De Gruyter (2023). https://doi.org/10.1515/9783110791402-014
52. Reddy, A.R.P., Ayyadapu, A.K.R.: Automating incident response: AI-driven approaches to cloud security incident management. Chelonian Res. Found. **15**(2), 1–10 (2020)
53. Sáez, C., Ferri, P., García-Gómez, J.M.: Resilient artificial intelligence in health: synthesis and research agenda toward next-generation trustworthy clinical decision support. J. Med. Internet Res. **26**, e50295 (2024)
54. Saraswat, D., et al.: Explainable ai for healthcare 5.0: opportunities and challenges. IEEE Access **10**, 84486–84517 (2022)
55. Seh, A.H., et al.: Healthcare data breaches: insights and implications. In: Healthcare. vol. 8, p. 133. MDPI (2020)
56. Shaheen, M.Y.: Applications of artificial intelligence (ai) in healthcare: A review. ScienceOpen Preprints (2021)
57. Shukla, A., Katt, B., Nweke, L.O., Yeng, P.K., Weldehawaryat, G.K.: System security assurance: a systematic literature review. Comput. Sci. Rev. **45**, 100496 (2022)

58. Sidhu, G.S., Sayem, M.A., Taslima, N., Anwar, A.S., Chowdhury, F., Rowshon, M.: Ai and workforce development: a comparative analysis of skill gaps and training needs in emerging economies. Int. J. Business Manage. Sci. **4**(08), 12–28 (2024)
59. Sinha, R.: The role and impact of new technologies on healthcare systems. Disc. Health Syst. **3**(1), 96 (2024)
60. Smith, H.: Clinical AI: opacity, accountability, responsibility and liability. AI Society **36**(2), 535–545 (2021)
61. Stevens, A.F., Stetson, P.: Theory of trust and acceptance of artificial intelligence technology (traait): An instrument to assess clinician trust and acceptance of artificial intelligence. J. Biomed. Inform. **148**, 104550 (2023)
62. Syed, F.M., ES, F.K., Johnson, E.: Ai-driven threat intelligence in healthcare cybersecurity. Revista de Inteligencia Artificial en Medicina **14**(1), 431–459 (2023)
63. Tagde, P., Tagde, S., Bhattacharya, T., Tagde, P., Chopra, H., Akter, R., Kaushik, D., Rahman, M.H.: Blockchain and artificial intelligence technology in e-health. Environ. Sci. Pollut. Res. **28**, 52810–52831 (2021)
64. Tervoort, T., De Oliveira, M.T., Pieters, W., Van Gelder, P., Olabarriaga, S.D., Marquering, H.: Solutions for mitigating cybersecurity risks caused by legacy software in medical devices: a scoping review. IEEE access **8**, 84352–84361 (2020)
65. Tong, W., Zhang, X., Zeng, H., Pan, J., Gong, C., Zhang, H.: Reforming china's secondary vocational medical education: adapting to the challenges and opportunities of the ai era. JMIR Med. Educ. **10**, e48594 (2024)
66. Tsvetanov, F.: Integrating AI technologies into remote monitoring patient systems. Eng. Proceed. **70**(1), 54 (2024)
67. s Vishwakarma, L.P., Singh, R.K., Mishra, R., Kumari, A.: Application of artificial intelligence for resilient and sustainable healthcare system: systematic literature review and future research directions. Int. J. Product. Res. 1–23 (2023)
68. Waheeb, R.: Improving healthcare centers' risk management by using ai. Available at SSRN 4862674 (2024)
69. Wen, S.F., Shukla, A., Katt, B.: Artificial intelligence for system security assurance: a systematic literature review. Int. J. Inf. Secur. **24**(1), 1–42 (2025)
70. Williamson, S.M., Prybutok, V.: Balancing privacy and progress: a review of privacy challenges, systemic oversight, and patient perceptions in AI-driven healthcare. Appl. Sci. **14**(2), 675 (2024)
71. Ye, J., Woods, D., Jordan, N., Starren, J.: The role of artificial intelligence for the application of integrating electronic health records and patient-generated data in clinical decision support. AMIA Summits Transl. Sci. Proceed. **2024**, 459 (2024)
72. Yeng, P.K., Nweke, L.O., Woldaregay, A.Z., Yang, B., Snekkenes, E.A.: Data-driven and artificial intelligence (AI) approach for modelling and analyzing healthcare security practice: a systematic review. In: Arai, K., Kapoor, S., Bhatia, R. (eds.) Intelligent Systems and Applications: Proceedings of the 2020 Intelligent Systems Conference (IntelliSys) Volume 1, pp. 1–18. Springer International Publishing, Cham (2021). https://doi.org/10.1007/978-3-030-55180-3_1
73. Zohuri, B., Rahmani, F.M.: Artificial intelligence driven resiliency with machine learning and deep learning components. Japan J. Res. **1**(1) (2023)

Author Index

A
Abie, Habtamu 3, 23

B
Baig, Ahmed Fraz 67
Barik, Kousik 87
Bours, Patrick 67

C
Chockalingam, Sabarathinam 23, 87

E
Eskeland, Sigurd 67

I
Iqbal, Muhammad Javed 45

K
Kaliyar, Pallavi 23

M
Misra, Sanjay 87
Mughal, Muhammad Irfan Younas 45

P
Pirbhulal, Sandeep 3, 23

S
Shukla, Ankur 109
Sodhro, Ali Hassan 45

X
Xu, Shouhuai 3

Y
Yang, Bian 67

The manufacturer's authorised representative in the EU is Springer Nature Customer Service Centre GmbH, Europaplatz 3, 69115 Heidelberg, Germany. If you have any concerns regarding our products, please contact ProductSafety@springernature.com

Printed and bound by CPI Group (UK) Ltd, Croydon, CR0 4YY

26/03/2026

02078935-0017